PSYCHICAL PHENOMENA

IS VOLUME

36

OF THE

Twentieth Century Encyclopedia of Catholicism

UNDER SECTION

III

THE NATURE OF MAN

IT IS ALSO THE

7TH

VOLUME IN ORDER OF PUBLICATION

Edited by HENRI DANIEL-ROPS of the Académie Française

PSYCHICAL PHENOMENA

By REGINALD OMEZ, O.P.

Translated from the French by RENÉE HAYNES

HAWTHORN BOOKS · PUBLISHERS · *New York*

 This book was manufactured in the United States of America and published simultaneously in Canada by McClelland & Stewart, Ltd., 25 Hollinger Road, Toronto 16. Original French edition, *Supranormal ou Surnatural?: Les Sciences Métapsychiques* © F. Brouty, J. Fayard et Cie, 1956. The Library of Congress has catalogued The Twentieth Century Encyclopedia of Catholicism under card number 58–14327.

First Edition, December, 1958

NIHIL OBSTAT

Andreas Moore, L.C.L.

Censor Deputatus

IMPRIMATUR

E. Morrogh Bernard

Vicarius Generalis

Westmonasterii, die XVII JULII MCMLVIII

The Library of Congress has catalogued this publication as follows:

Omez, Reginald, 1895–

Psychical phenomena. Translated from the French by Renée Haynes. New York, Hawthorn Books [1958]

144 p. 21 cm. (The Twentieth century encyclopedia of Catholicism, v. 36. Section 3: The nature of man)

Translation of Supranormal ou surnaturel? Les sciences métapsychiques. Bibliography: p. [142]–144.

1. Psychical research. I. Title. (Series: The Twentieth century encyclopedia of Catholicism, v. 36)

BF1032.O513 133.072 58–11598

CONTENTS

TRANSLATOR'S PREFACE

Translators are traitors, says the Italian proverb. To make a translation is to become guiltily and increasingly aware of its inevitable truth. Translators *must* be traitors, either to the author or to the reader in whose language they write. The best they can hope for is to avoid the double treachery of misrepresenting the one *and* misleading the other.

This is so because an original work, even if written in a European language and tradition, is not simply a series of words, sentences and paragraphs, for which English equivalents must be found. It is a product of history, cultural and national and specific. Its historical matrix will not only affect its idiom, style and construction; it will also condition the way in which it is thought out. Thus—as has happened in the present instance—the French writer will think much more in terms of abstract ideas and logical categories than his English counterpart; and if what he writes be translated into the strict equivalents in our language the average English reader, accustomed to an empirical tradition, will need to make a constant effort to use an unexercised set of intellectual muscles before he can even begin to absorb ideas presented to him. I have therefore from time to time ventured to translate not only words but concepts, so that, for instance, "verify the reality of such phenomena" may be rendered as "investigate whether such phenomena do in fact occur" ("reality" being to our ears rather a question-begging term). Verbal nouns have here and there replaced abstract ones, and -ing has been given priority over -ation.

In order not to interrupt the flow of the work I have occasionally incorporated one or two sentences showing where

English or American usages or findings differ to a marked degree from those of France. Where, however, the difference is one of principle, comments have been made in the form of translator's notes, mostly at the foot of the page, but in one or two cases in brackets in the body of the text.

The chief source of such differences is probably historical. Parapsychology in France seems to have developed on lines very unlike those it has followed here. There it has been continually entangled with theories, from the time of the so-called *Miraculés* of Port Royal to that of the ingenious Mesmer (whose memory grows green in the tendency to attribute success in water-divining and faith-cures to some mysterious "electric fluid") and on to Napoleon III with his passion for clairvoyants, fortune-tellers, and the flights, bangs and tambourine performances of Douglas Home. Here, since the foundation of the Society for Psychical Research in 1882 by a group of Cambridge scientists and philosophers, psychical research has been based on the collection, verification and evaluation of data and the organization of experimental work. Though many interested in the subject have also been interested in what our author calls "occultism" (roughly the theory and practice of spiritualism, with its reliance on mediums, *séances*, "spirit guides", spirit healing etc.; and the teachings of Theosophy, Christian Science and other forms of Gnosticism) in the day to day work of the Society objective study has never yielded place to the overriding desire to use *psi*-phenomena simply as theory-fodder. The Society does not commit itself to any collective opinion.

In England, therefore, there has been little of that need to define the subject against recurrent jungle growths of parasitic cosmologies which is so plainly to be observed in these pages. Here, moreover, there is not such a marked tendency as there is in France to erect as it were notice boards marked TRESPASSERS WILL BE PROSECUTED between one field of study and another; we have no academic conscience to prevent our picking up gold and silver on Tom Tiddler's ground, if it is there for the taking, and should not commit ourselves to statements implying that parapsychology and philosophy must work in watertight compartments.

Such an academic conscience is probably responsible for the omission of a cardinal point in the otherwise most interesting passages on the usefulness and significance of parapsychology. It is this.

As the author suggests, the *psi*-function at work in telepathy and precognition may indeed be a rudimentary survival of a power more fully operative among animals and primitive human tribes than in contemporary urban civilizations (compare the power to move one's ears). It is also arguable that it is potentially present among them all, but that its emergence and development, like those of other psychological functions, are deeply conditioned, sometimes even inhibited, by the culture pattern, the circumstances and the personal history of each individual. In either case, the fact that it exists, and has been proved to exist, shows the necessity of envisaging a world in which consciousness is not, as posited by nineteenth-century materialist philosophers in Europe and their twentieth-century successors in Russia, simply an epiphenomenon, an inevitable but meaningless accompaniment of physical processes: that the psyche is at some level capable of transcending time and space if only in flashes and to an infinitesimal degree; and that the human psyche, made in the image of God, and reflexively conscious of itself can both realize the existence of these capacities and understand what they imply about its own nature and that of the universe.

Though the existence of the *psi*-function has been established in the context not of theology but of biology, it clearly opens a way out of the intellectual prison of materialist philosophy for those who have hitherto believed that regard for objective truth must lock them in. One proof of this is the fury aroused in Marxian scientists by the work of Rhine upon which, with that of Soal and Bateman, the statistical proofs are based.

To Catholics inhabiting a religious climate of thought these considerations may seem unimportant; but to those,

Catholics or otherwise, whose lives interact continually with a world that accepts materialism so deeply that it has no need to formulate its tenets, it is extraordinarily stimulating to observe, for the first time since the Renaissance, a scientific discipline discovering and defining in its own language even part of a truth long reiterated in terms now unfamiliar to the greater part of mankind.

RENÉE HAYNES

Epiphany, 1958

INTRODUCTION

DOES A SCIENCE OF PARAPSYCHOLOGY REALLY EXIST?

The question above was put to me by M. Daniel-Rops, the general editor of this series, designed for a wide public. Because of this, the reply which I shall attempt to give in this book will not be meant for specialists in psychical research, but for every reader who is or who might be interested in the problem.

My first concern will be to formulate, as far as may be, the significance of the term parapsychology, which may be quite obscure or even wholly meaningless to some readers. The time has not yet come for an exact and exhaustive definition of parapsychology, mapping out its subject matter and indicating the methods that it should use; we shall hardly get to that stage even at the end of our search. For the moment let us confine ourselves to indicating in an approximate and provisional way the content of the question that has been put.

Parapsychology as a scientific discipline—whose very existence has been queried—is concerned to investigate those unusual, strange, mysterious phenomena which go beyond the normal, known powers of the human soul or psyche, and seem to imply the action either of entities superior to that soul or of some unfamiliar factor within it. Parapsychological phenomena will be taken to include all those involved in the marvellous in the widest sense; whether they occur in the context of religion, spiritualism, occultism, diabolism, psychology, physics, chemistry or physiology.

It is easy to form some idea of the enormous extent of this field; think of the activities attributed to the dead, of apparitions and visions of all kinds, of spiritualist manifestations; add to these paranormal healing, telepathy, thought-reading, clairvoyance, psychometry, radiesthesia (dowsing, water divining, medical dowsing), predictions and premonitions, astrology; and then again the phenomena of levitation, the "apports" of people and things, the stories of haunted houses, magic, and so on.

Contemporary journalism keeps us amply informed of such events, and is always successful in so doing, for public curiosity is invariably avid for everything which seems strange and mysterious. There is a spate of articles in newspapers and periodicals, and even of expensive books, which attempt to prove that entities superior to man really intervene in his life, or to establish that there exist in man himself unknown powers in whose activity is to be found the true explanation of apparently marvellous events.

What is the value of these hypotheses, some postulating the existence of alien hidden spirit forces, divine or diabolical, others based on a critical rationalism which completely denies all possibility of action by preternatural entities? Another question inevitably arises; are there really any trustworthy people, genuine scientists, unprejudiced philosophers, who take an interest in these strange phenomena and attempt to find out first whether they do in fact occur, and then whether it is possible to discover their origins and their causes, natural or supernatural?

The first thing is to define once and for all what is meant by parapsychology. For, if parapsychology, the paranormal and psychical research are much discussed, the words tend to become blunted, and even to be used in self-contradictory senses. These terms have indeed been so misused that it is often almost impossible to guess how much they are intended to cover. We note that the heading "parapsychologists" includes sometimes genuine experts, psychologists versed in their special subject and wisely critical of the material presented to them, sometimes occultists, spiritualists, mediums, clairvoyants and fortune-tellers, not to speak of impostors, hysterical liars, and abnormal personalities of all kinds. This in France. In Britain it is only those who are completely ignorant of the subject who confuse psychical research with cosmological theories or commercial practices; though it is obviously necessary, in the nature of things, for psychical research workers to use for their investigations the data provided by those involved in these proliferating ideologies and activities.

The expression "psychic" has in both countries acquired so discreditable an overtone that it often arouses distaste or a derisory smile not only in scientists and philosophers but also in the majority of sensible educated people. Even the title of this book may leave many reflecting that the subject is hardly worth consideration.

I hold, on the contrary, that now is an opportune moment at which to formulate it, and to try to find an answer; and I am convinced that those who have the patience to read this book to the end will agree that the problem was well worth discussion even though the solution has not yet been completely worked out, and there are a number of points on which judgement must remain in suspense.

ETYMOLOGY AND TERMINOLOGY

M. Robert Amadou, in his important book *La Parapsychologie* ("Parapsychology"),[1] retraces (p. 13) the development of the expressions metapsychic, metapsychology, parapsychology, parapsychic, etc. In theory it should not matter much which term is used for preference. All these words have the same root, and pretty well the same meaning. "Meta" and "para" indicate a "going beyond" some frontier into an unknown region. "Psychic" and "psychological" too, should be two words for one concept: the life, powers and activities of the human soul. It is an historical matter of group-usage that has come to make the employment of the

[1] Denoël, 1954.

former denote a spiritualist attitude while the latter remains an ordinary scientific term.

"Metapsychics" or "Parapsychology" should then be equivalent words used to denote psychological events which seem to go beyond the normal, recognized, everyday activities of the psyche, providing evidence which seems inexplicable except in terms either of the intervention of some entity other than ourselves or of the play of some function other than our known faculties and the senses recognized by contemporary physiology.

Such, then, is the etymological sense, the primitive content of such expressions as metapsychic, parapsychological, and so on. In this book we shall try to use terms that are as far as possible neutral, rendering for instance "metapsychics" as "parapsychology" or "psychical research". It is good to know that an international group of investigators is at work upon an agreed list of terms and definitions for use in this field.

TERMINOLOGICAL MISUSE

In France the word "metapsychic" (like "psychic" in England) has often been used derogatively to indicate phenomena, teachings and hypotheses which have little to do with the objective sphere of genuine scientific investigation. The epithet has been applied to the most chimerical theories of occultism and spiritualism, and to the whole realm of dreams and delusions where fraud and hysterical romancing take root and flourish royally. We shall see later that such aberrations have played some part even in those groups founded to study parapsychology whose rules seemed to ensure an objective outlook; for rational and scientific investigators rub shoulders in these groups with fellow members of little standing, who lack all critical sense.

In his book *La Métapsychique de 1940 à 1946* ("Parapsychology from 1940 to 1946")[1], Professor William Mackenzie justly complains about "the obstinate confusion

[1] *Presses Universitaires de France.*

which many still make between parapsychology and spiritualism". Parapsychologists have sometimes been responsible for this confusion, in their whole-hearted acceptance of the help given to them by spiritualists and others who are incapable of devoting themselves objectively to the study of paranormal phenomena.[1]

Professor Mackenzie is certainly sincere when he writes: "Our science wishes to observe, without preconceived ideas. Before anything else, it needs to verify the occurrence of phenomena. Then it must experiment as widely as possible with a view to discovering and establishing what conditions are necessary if they are to be produced. Deductions must be made from these experiments, and sequences of events, correspondences of evidence, and eventual constants must be noted. Finally the phenomena themselves must be classified, and newly observed evidence should if possible be related to the categories in which known facts have already been grouped. All lies in this." Agreed; but it is also necessary to discard colleagues who wish to exploit the work of psychical research groups for the purposes of propaganda on behalf of this or that little sect. Unless this is done, serious students will inevitably be tempted to reject the achievements of such groups *en bloc,* confusing work of real value with evidence obtained under conditions where no control could be exercised, and with the imaginative phantasies built upon this shifting sand.

These first explorations of the meaning of our question have already shown its importance and its possibilities. It is clearly necessary that the educated public should know where it stands in face of the reports of marvellous occurrences which appear in the press, and of the various theories,

[1] It must in justice be regognized that their position has been a difficult one. Scientists cannot work without guinea-pigs; and those human guinea-pigs in whom the requisite abilities occur tend, like those gifted in music, drama, etc., to be incapable of such objectivity. They are not usually scholars or scientists but artists uninterested in, and often incapable of, the detached analysis of their own abilities. [*Trans.*]

scientific and otherwise, which are put forward to explain them.

Is there a genuine science of the marvellous? Are there genuine research workers who recognize and test the evidence for these occurrences, and rough out explanations of them, explanations which, if not complete, are at any rate worthy of the attention of readers anxious not to be taken in by the illusions and deliberate frauds which are all too common in this field? To discover this is the object of this book.

After having looked into the question of whether psychical research exists as a scientific discipline, and whether those engaged in it are genuinely scholarly in their approach, we shall try to assemble the proven results of their investigations. Having sorted out the results of trickery, and all phenomena susceptible of a natural explanation, we shall ask the experts in parapsychology whether they have indeed been able to verify the occurrence of events which cannot be accounted for in terms of what is at present known about the powers of the human soul, the human organism in general. In the face of such evidence as has been solidly tested, can they maintain that we possess certain unexplored or little-known faculties as would explain paranormal occurrences where they cannot be attributed to the activity of discarnate beings or to a miraculous intervention of God himself?

By definition, the supernatural slips through the mesh of parapsychology as of other sciences. All they can do is to affirm or deny the existence of the paranormal. It is for philosophy[1] or theology to trace the origin of what lies beyond the resources of nature.

After this critical assessment of the current data of psychical research we shall examine the question of whether these discoveries open up interesting prospects for the future, and promise to enrich the psyche, or whether the functions they reveal seem to be in the nature of palaeontological fossils, the more or less conscious remains of primitive instincts

[1] But surely philosophy must be concerned to integrate evidence of all kinds in a unity of knowledge. [*Trans.*]

atrophied during the course of human evolution, and infinitely surpassed in usefulness by the progress of contemporary knowledge, communication and action.

The topicality of our question is shown by the appearance during the last few years of various works examining the same problem from different angles. The titles of the most important will be found in the Bibliography, which also gives the names of a number of standard works.

CHAPTER I

AN HISTORICAL SKETCH

We cannot hope to trace the history of psychical research in detail. It would need considerable digression, which would be irritating to the majority of readers. We must be content to record some significant stages which will help us more easily to grasp the nature and the current development of the work whose value we must try to determine.

Long before our time, psychologists observed phenomena whose strangeness and mystery seemed to spring from other causes, and to need other explanations, than the working of the faculties traditionally attributed to the human soul. While the usual tendency was to envisage these phenomena as the work of discarnate entities, souls in heaven, or purgatory or hell, angels or demons, there were scholars and philosophers who thought it possible that there might be a natural explanation to be found for some paranormal cases, believing that the human soul possessed certain qualities still not yet understood, certain powers beyond those which had so far been analysed and established.

In connection with supposed cases of diabolical possession or obsession, various theologians and Benedict XIV himself (1740-58) had already drawn the attention of both exorcists and doctors to the extraordinary, and apparently diabolical, phenomena which might arise from psychological illness. He declared that "doctors themselves diagnose many people as obsessed (that is to say, tormented by the devil) who are not".

It was not until towards the end of the nineteenth century

that methodical research was organized to investigate the origin and nature of certain paranormal phenomena attributed to human energy of a kind that had not so far been recognized. We see, for instance, Emile Boirac, in *La Psychologie inconnue* ("Unknown Psychology") which appeared in 1908, reprinting various articles published between 1893 and 1903, which discussed phenomena that he labelled "parapsychological".

CHARLES RICHET

While in England Gurney, Myers, Crookes and others had laid the foundation of the new science a good deal earlier, in France these special studies were made known to the general public, as well as to philosophical circles, by Charles Richet's famous book *Le Traité de Métapsychique*, published in 1922, which appeared in English as *Thirty Years of Psychical Research*. In this learned work the author attempted first to define the dawning science, and then to describe its various objects and its untried hypotheses, in two sections entitled: (1) Subjective Parapsychology and (2) Objective Parapsychology. (These terms have now been dropped.)

His intention was to undertake a strictly scientific piece of work. In the preface he made a statement all too often forgotten: "Those who hope to find in this book a number of cloudy speculations on human destiny, magic, and theosophy, will be disappointed. I have been concerned with trying to write a work of science, not of dreams. I have therefore confined myself to setting out the facts and discussing their authenticity, not only without offering a theory of my own but without much reference to any theories at all; for those which have so far been formulated in parapsychology seem to me alarmingly fragile. It is possible, even probable, that a useful theory may some day be put forward. But that time has not yet come, since the actual facts on which to build a theory are still in question. It is therefore first of all essential to establish those facts, and to present them in general and in detail, so that their background may be fully understood. This is our first duty; even our sole duty."

Who would not endorse these words of a true scholar, critical and cautious? But alas, it is not surprising that, through a misfortune constantly recurrent in the history of human thought, the readers and disciples of Charles Richet came to lose sight of these sensible warnings, and abandoned both his moderation and his critical standards. Disciples sometimes become destroyers.

After this introduction to his theme Richet enumerated three categories of phenomena which seemed to him to constitute the legitimate subject-matter of the new field of research. He grouped them under three provisional headings, intended, as he clearly indicated, rather to sort out the evidence to be tested than to explain its significance.

1. Clairvoyance (the "lucidity" referred to by ancient writers): "that is, a faculty of perception different from the normal sensory faculties". Richet affirmed its existence: for him man was in fact gifted with a "supernormal faculty"; clairvoyance, "second sight". He instanced a very large number of cases in which this faculty is exemplified.

2. "Telekinesis: that is, a form of physical action different from any known mechanical forces, which could be exerted without contact and at a distance, under certain conditions, on persons or material objects."

3. "The production of ectoplasm (termed 'materialization' by older writers on the subject); that is to say the formation of various objects from a substance which most frequently seems to proceed from the human body, and takes on the appearance of material reality (clothes, veils, living bodies)."

Such were the manifestations whose authenticity Richet set himself to investigate. He defined this new branch of science as "a science whose object it is to study those phenomena, physical or psychological, due to forces which seem intelligent, or to latent unknown powers in the human mind".

In his methods of working he aimed above all at establishing a critical verification of the evidence. "It is no longer permissible to allow a medium to produce phenomena before an amateur and restricted circle, without having recourse to the research methods in constant use in other scientific work; scales, photography, cinephotography and so on." "The time has not yet come for synthesis; we must get on with analysis first."

Nevertheless Charles Richet was already noting, very rightly, that a prerequisite of the phenomena attributed to mediums is a kind of dilution of psychological consciousness. "Mediums are individuals, partly or wholly unconscious, who say words, make gestures, carry out actions: words, gestures, actions which seem dissociated from their will, and appear to be independent of their intelligence. Nevertheless, these unconscious phenomena are intelligent and systematic, and sometimes coordinated with remarkable insight. Hence, from the outset it is necessary to discover whether these unconscious phenomena are due to a human or to a superhuman intelligence."

This was already a definition of the indispensable preliminaries to all parapsychological problems. It orientated scientific research towards the analysis of the unconscious—or I should prefer to say the subconscious—in order to discover to what extent this unconscious could explain phenomena which seemed to surpass or at any rate to elude the powers of the normal conscious mind.

Richet cited, of course, the known cases of dual personality, recalling that this phenomenon was recognized by normal classical psychology. In connection with automatic writing he noted moreover that "there is no need to classify this important psychological manifestation under the heading of parapsychology, for the hypothesis of a non-human intelligence is irrelevant in the majority of cases".

Given the incalculable richness of the unconscious mind, which might well account more or less completely for a large proportion of apparently paranormal events, Richet set himself to examine the evidence for occurrences which seemed obviously to go beyond the powers of that unconscious. He gave especial attention to physical phenomena (levitation, poltergeist hauntings, telekinesis, materialization). It was there that he hoped to find something "new, transcendental, really parapsychological" and to discover unknown energies belonging either to the human soul or to discarnate entities.

He undertook this task with the still very limited techniques, the fairly rudimentary instruments of the experimental sciences of his time. His book will remain above all—it devotes 700 pages to the theme—a collection of hundreds of cases which seem to manifest paranormal modes of knowledge, activity and materialization. Since then, possibilities of control have developed incomparably. Scientific and technical discoveries today allow of much more rigorous laboratory conditions. And Richet's "really parapsychological" physical phenomena have little by little been eliminated or at any rate whittled down.

It is nevertheless instructive to note the conclusions reached by this pioneer of French psychical research. They are modest enough: "We are working in an unknown field. Nevertheless we have been able to establish beyond reasonable doubt the existence of two great facts. (1) That the human mind has other means of knowledge than the normal senses: clairvoyance, the *psi*-factor. (2) That materialization, that is, the emergence from the body of forces which can take on a physical form and then behave as if they were material objects, does indeed occur. It does not seem to me that one can go further than clairvoyance and materialization, without losing oneself in the clouds. How many stories have I heard, told by witnesses of the most complete good faith, whose observations have been made with more enthusiasm than critical sense." Among the data of clairvoyance Richet included verified presentiments or premonitions, and among the data of materialization some of the phenomena of telekinesis and levitation.

He could discover no satisfactory explanation of these facts.

He discounted the spiritualist theory of intervention by discarnate beings. He reacted strongly against those who wished to elucidate parapsychology by esoteric religious propositions. "The spiritualists want to mix up religion with science, to the great disadvantage of science. They have swaddled their séances with 'mystagoguery', saying prayers as if they were in a chapel . . . convinced that they were conversing with the dead, losing themselves in infantile elaborations. . . . They have drowned themselves in childish theologies and theosophies."

The desire for dissociation from all spiritualist doctrines is very clearly affirmed.

Doubtless Charles Richet supported his views by spiritualist data; but it was only as a scholarly observer, who completely rejected the hypotheses put forward by the various spiritualist schools. He frequently used the term "medium" but did not accept its spiritualist connotations. "The word medium, execrable as it is, is common parlance. It is impossible to get rid of it." For him mediums were in no way intermediaries between this world and the "beyond"; they were no more than persons with a remarkable gift for projecting the products of the unconscious mind. "Naïvely, we take it for granted that we are hearing the words of a discarnate entity, whereas in fact we are overhearing the turmoil of the subconscious mind, crystallized around a fictitious personality"; and again: "If one accepted Allan Kardec's theory one would have to accept at their face value all the wanderings of the unconscious which without exception bear witness to a very primitive and childish intelligence. It is a very great mistake to found a doctrine upon the words of those self-styled spirits who are so dim-witted." One could hardly be more stinging to those spiritualists with whom Charles Richet was so constantly in touch.

After having outlined three hypotheses: (1) the intervention of the dead, (2) the activity of angels and demons, (3) a power of producing *psi*-manifestations inherent in human intelligence, Richet adds (p. 790): "For my own part, I wholeheartedly adopt a fourth proposition, which has every chance of turning out to be true; it is that we have not yet any reliable hypothesis to put forward. I believe in an unknown hypothesis of the future, which I cannot formulate because I do not know it." We return to our starting point, to that most sensible maxim which psychical research students cannot too often remember and put into practice: "If we wish parapsychology to be a science, let us begin by establishing the facts on a firm basis. I do not doubt that our successors will go farther than this, but our task today is a humbler one. Let us maintain that prudence and caution which befit ignorance."

His efforts towards assembling, with the help of competent and critical scholars, a collection of observations and experiments organized in accordance with his concept of parapsychology, and with his criteria of judgement, ended in disappointment. He tried to found, with T. Ribot and L. Marillier, a "Society for Physiological Psychology". It was a failure. He acknowledged it in these words: "We had the vexatious idea of trying to interest psychologists, physiologists, doctors, in psychical research. They would never consent to take it seriously."

Later he founded with Dariex *Les Annales des sciences psychiques* ("Annals of Psychic Science", 1890-1920) which was succeeded by *La Revue métapsychique* ("Parapsychological Review") founded by Dr G. Geley. Of this last he hoped that it would be "a just balance between the credulity of spiritualist papers and the blind ignorance of the official periodicals dealing with psychology". We shall refer to it again.

Richet had recognized and maintained the necessity, even for the most serious students of psychical research—who could not, he thought, be more than "isolated individuals"—to keep in close touch with the so-called psychic societies, whose members sought mediumistic experiments often very much more for the sake of curiosity or emotional satisfaction than in any scientific spirit. "In fact, there can be no parapsychology without a medium. The duty of psychical research societies is, precisely, not to allow the powers of certain remarkable mediums to fizzle out without any profit to science in the obscurity of amateurish *séances* undertaken without strict safeguards against fraud." The necessity of retaining a welcoming attitude towards these various societies of mediums and their spirit-guides led to a serious danger; that of being drowned in the flood of the curious, the naïve, the "enlightened", the partisans always attracted by this sort of mysterious and slightly sinister business. The snag could not be completely avoided. Such circles were inevitably a battlefield for two different groups, one scientific, the other occultist and spiritualist. It is practically impossible in societies of this kind completely to exclude unbalanced people, charlatans seeking notoriety, mythomaniacs, hysterics, and so forth, who diminish the value of such groups in the eyes of conscientious research workers, and arouse repulsion in critical scholars.

THE INTERNATIONAL METAPSYCHICAL INSTITUTE

This was founded in 1919, thanks to the financial help of Jean Meyer, who gave it a large building in the Avenue Niel, Paris. The generous donor was himself "a militant spiritualist", so we are assured in *La Revue métapsychique* for July 1955. He edited *La Revue spirite* ("Spiritualist Review") for fifteen years.

Charles Richet was doubtless its chief inspiration, but the direction was in the main in the hands of Dr G. Geley from 1919 to 1924, and in those of Dr Osty from 1925 to 1938. Its present president is M. Warcollier, a chemical engineer.

Its articles of association stated that the aim of this Institute was "to enable scientific persons to undertake a methodical study of all apparently paranormal phenomena, without any preconceived theory and without any aim except the accumulation of evidence and the discovery of truth".

Financial difficulties obliged the Institute to cut down its activities. In 1954 it sold its original premises and moved to more modest accommodation at 1 Place Wagram, Paris.

Among its best-known contemporary members we should at least mention Dr Henri Desoille, Professor at the Faculty of Medicine of Paris, Dr Vinchon, formerly head of a clinic in the Paris hospitals, Mrs Eileen Garrett, president of the Parapsychology Foundation of New York, and Professor Gardner Murphy, chairman of the department of psychology at the City College of New York, and a former president of the Society for Psychical Research in England.

Many were the activities of this scientific group; from experimental *séances* (where a limited number of specialists checked and analysed the paranormal material furnished by mediums, automatic painters, thought transmitters, clairvoyants, etc.) to lectures open to the general public, and to the publication of books and periodicals, some of which had a great success. In spite of the limited scope of this study, we cannot leave unmentioned the *séances* conducted with Eusapia Palladino, nor the remarkable work carried out by M. René Warcollier in the field of telepathy. We shall have the opportunity of putting on record some of the results of this scientific research.

LA REVUE METAPSYCHIQUE

This was the most appreciated of the activities of the International Metapsychical Institute, the one which contributed most to its reputation, and made it known to educated circles, the majority of which would never have had any other contact with it. This monthly review, founded in 1920 by Dr G. Geley, published over some twenty years articles on the doctrine, or rather the theory, of psychical research, and, most important of all, descriptions of experiments and observations. It is easy to imagine how hard it must have been to ensure the regular appearance of such a bulletin, and to cover its expenses.

After the interruption due to the war, the review reappeared in 1948. Dr F. Moutier, in an article on the rational approach to parapsychology, acknowledged that in the mass of material recorded by the International Metapsychical Institute "an irritating proportion of chaff is mixed with the grain". But he made clear in the name of the editorial board how much care had been taken to examine the abundant documentary evidence amassed over thirty years and to devise methods and techniques of control which should ensure accuracy. He wished that an effort could be made to renew psychical research work in a rational and objective spirit. After this the Review became rather more specialized, devoting attention (1) to data connected with psycho-kinesis, that is, the proposition that a human personality may be able directly to affect some material object without physical contact, without the use of any instrument, and without the exercise of any method of transmitting energy at present known to science, (2) to data tending to establish the reality of extra-sensory, or parapsychological, perception; telepathy, clairvoyance, dowsing, etc.

After various ups and downs the Review faced a serious situation in 1955. Its editor-in-chief, M. Robert Amadou, had left it and founded a new periodical, while the International Metapsychical Institute, under the direction of M. Warcollier and M. F. Masse, launched in July of that year the first number of a new series. Henceforward *La Revue Métapsychique* appeared three times a year and published nothing but accounts of research work. Its new and more austere set-up quite certainly lost it some readers; but it attracted others with higher critical standards.

L'ASSOCIATION FRANÇAISE D'ETUDES METAPSYCHIQUES

The French Association for Parapsychological Studies was founded on October 15th, 1941, by the Vicomte B. de Cressac Bachelerie, an engineer, and a former vice-president of the

Committee for Studies of the International Metapsychical Institute. It had many well-known members.

Its programme was to group together technicians, doctors and scholars anxious to advance the study of psychical research in accordance with strictly scientific methods, and without any political, philosophical or religious preconceptions.

The Association could not avoid the inevitable snag already discussed; among its members were the presidents of two spiritualist groups in Paris. It was in close touch with one publishing firm which produced the periodical *L'Initiation-Magie-Science* whose title speaks for itself, and with another devoted chiefly to the production of books with a spiritualist and occultist flavour.

THE "CAHIERS METAPSYCHIQUES"

After having planned to launch a review *Sciences Métapsychiques* ("Parapsychological Science") the Association brought out in January 1950 the first of a series, *Cahiers Métapsychiques* ("Parapsychological Bulletins"). This periodical, appearing thrice a year, contained contributions of very uneven merit, on parapsychology, astrology and various esoteric themes.

The interesting experimental researches designed to demonstrate the existence of telepathy, and to further the study of "psychokinetic effects" should be noted. Thanks to an ingenius apparatus invented by M. Chevalier, an engineer, an attempt was made to establish whether the *psi*-factor could affect the free flow of drops of water on to the blade of a knife, set up vertically. The apparatus was gradually perfected so as to eliminate all other factors capable of influencing the flow or of producing the slightest deviation of each drop. The idea on which the experiment was based was certainly worth continued attention. But after several years of work the results were still inconclusive.

J. B. RHINE

The influence exerted by this professor of Duke University, Durham, N. C., on the study of parapsychology throughout the world means that several pages must be devoted to his work, in spite of the need to make this historical survey as brief as possible. For Rhine has set psychical research on a new path, not indeed by putting some hitherto unsuspected question, nor by using methods previously unknown, but by his more scientific mode of formulating the problem of whether the phenomena of extra-sensory perception really occur, and by the strictly mathematical methods he has used to test such phenomena.

While the majority of parapsychologists had rather hastily taken it for granted that the facts of extra-sensory perception were scientifically established, and occupied themselves primarily in attempting to explain their origin and the conditions favourable to their appearance, Rhine thought it essential to blot out all the explanations and hypotheses which had so far been put forward, and to start again from scratch, asking first of all: Do the phenomena of paranormal knowledge beyond the powers of the five known senses really exist? These phenomena, to which he refers by the initials E.S.P. (extra-sensory perception) are above all those of telepathy and clairvoyance.

To establish the objective existence of such facts as these, Rhine used two strictly critical methods of investigation. In the majority of instances these phenomena appear spontaneously without having been planned, and therefore without affording an opportunity for any fully satisfactory observation and control so that it is usually impossible to prove that apparent telepathy, or so-called thought transmission, are any more than striking coincidences, produced by capricious chance; or as the result of fraud or delusion; or the workings of the subconscious on data already known, interweaving unconscious associations with images of the past, etc. For this reason Rhine wished to accumulate statistical evidence of E.S.P. phenomena, easy to reproduce under laboratory conditions, so that he might later evaluate it in terms of the calculus of probabilities. Instead of stopping at the analysis, however performed, of a single event, which it was often impossible to prove, Rhine attempted to eliminate, mathematically so to speak, the hypothesis of a fortuitous coincidence which made other explanations unnecessary. He applied this quantitative method to the largest possible number of controlled experimental cases.

Secondly, in order to obviate all fraud, delusion, subconscious deception and so on, he set to work to investigate, by objective methods, every conceivable explanation of his data, before postulating the possibility of paranormal cognition.

The calculus of probabilities cannot with absolute certainty exclude the play of chance in small-scale experiments; that is why Rhine appealed to this second method to eliminate every conceivable alternative hypothesis. He reckons, however, that unless the record of successes, even extraordinary ones, in a series of experiments in thought-transmission is greater than the proportion of successes predictable by the calculus of probability they cannot scientifically be attributed to any cause but chance.

THE ZENER CARDS

In order to construct this statistical foundation to his work, Dr Rhine created a method of procedure so well known and so widely used in international psychical research that it seems essential to outline it here. It will show the reader the extent to which the new techniques of parapsychology have been worked out with a view to rigid objectivity.

In this experiment he uses Zener cards, named after Dr Zener who first designed them. There are twenty-five cards to a set, made up of five cards of each kind, a drawing on a white ground; one depicts a cross, another a circle, another a star, another a square, and another wavy lines. The cards are shuffled and cut in such a way that the pack of twenty-five is completely in random order, and it is impossible to guess the position of any one card. The person undertaking the experiment is then asked to name, in succession, the design of each of the cards, of which he will only see the back; and not always even that. Since there are only five kinds of card it is plain that the person concerned has one chance in five of picking on the right card through sheer luck. Thus on twenty-five cards the chance average should be five. It can be imagined that luck can vary the proportion of successes if only a few experiments are undertaken; but if a large number are recorded this possibility is ruled out by the mathematical laws of the calculus of probability.

Rhine then consulted mathematicians, eminent specialists in statistics, in order to evaluate both his method and the results of his observations. These scientific authorities acknowledged that the procedure employed was a perfectly legitimate one, and quite conclusive from the mathematical point of view, assuming of course that from the psychological angle no factor existed which could distort the experiments. This was for instance the conclusion reached by the Congress of Statistical Mathematics held at Indianapolis in 1937.

These experiments were tried on a very large scale in 1938 when Dr Greenwood extended them to the number of five million. In addition to the quantitative development of research work, every effort was made to eliminate all those factors which might have falsified their results; all the methods or tricks which might possibly have facilitated any normal knowledge, by indirect means, of the picture on the card. The total results were of such a nature that it is now possible mathematically to confirm the existence of extra-sensory perception.

These experiments were modified and perfected by a considerable number of experts, in order to make their results increasingly significant. Without going into the details of all this research, we may note the conclusion expressed at the first Congress of International Parapsychology at Utrecht in 1953 by Dr Schaefer, Professor of Physics at the University of Heidelberg: "Parapsychology is still struggling to have the phenomena it studies recognized as what they are. For me, Rhine's experiments have established the reality of these phenomena as far as telepathy and clairvoyance are concerned."

In his book *La Parapsychologie* ("Parapsychology") M. Robert Amadou ends a study of the part played by Rhine and his followers with these words: "From the long history whose principal events we have just recalled, one certainty emerges, one certainty indeed imposes itself on the minds of even the most sceptical, the most legitimately anxious to maintain objective standards. It is the certainty that a fact exists. It is the certainty that a phenomenon, long suspected has at last been recognized as an established truth through the development of new methods in psychical research." A decisive stage in the history of parapsychology does indeed seem to have been passed.

AN INTERNATIONAL PARAPSYCHOLOGY CONFERENCE

This absolutely unprecedented event took place at the University of Utrecht from July 30th to August 5th, 1953, the first international meeting, attended by sixty-two delegates from fourteen nations: specialists in different academic disciplines, philosophical and scientific, physicists, chemists, biologists, doctors, psychologists, psychiatrists, engineers, mathematicians, astronomers. Their object was to set out and to compare the results of their research, and to attempt to formulate a few first principles in the realm of psychical research. The programme was vast; it dealt with problems of methodology; the qualitative appraisal of spontaneous cases; quantitative research; physiological studies; psychoanalytical studies; parapsychology; and philosophy.

As a result of these first general exchanges, the members of the conference decided on future meetings on a narrower basis, in order that specialists in various fields might work together on more limited problems. From this decision arose the two discussion meetings at Saint-Paul-de-Vence in April 1954. From the 20th to 26th April the relations between parapsychology and philosophy were discussed, and from the 26th to the 30th the theme was paranormal healing.

To give some idea of the importance and the quality of these exchanges of ideas, we must note that the first conference was directed by Professor H. H. Price, of Oxford, and by M. Gabriel Marcel, member of the Institut de France. We must also note that contributions were made by Dr F. Leuret, president of the *Bureau des Constatations Médicales de Lourdes,* who gave an account of the work done in checking up on cures; and by Dr Larcher, Fr Beirnaert, S.J., and others.

These first international meetings of scientists, scholars and philosophers marked a considerable development in parapsychological science, and a serious effort to dissociate it from occultist and spiritualist ideas. The account of these congresses published in 1955 by M. Robert Amadou is a convincing proof of this.

THE GROUP FOR PARAPSYCHOLOGICAL STUDIES

As a sequel to the meeting of Saint-Paul-de-Vence, a Group for Parapsychological Studies with the same outlook was formed in 1954 under the direction of M. Robert Amadou, M. Maurice Colinon and Dr Martiny. The number of its members was voluntarily restricted, there was no publicity, and the group was drawn from among members of the International Metapsychical Institute, and other experts whose recognized scientific achievements and high critical standards guaranteed that they had something of value to contribute. There were doctors, engineers, a few specialist clergy such as Abbé Oraison, Fr Louis Beirnaert, S.J., Fr Bruno de Jésus-Marie, O.C.D., and two Protestant ministers. Scientific objectivity precluded all thought of partisan feeling.

During the first year the group divided itself into four sections, which were assigned the following subjects of study: statistics and parapsychology; paranormal healing; physiology and parapsychology; parapsychology in ancient times.

The Group founded in November 1955 a *Bulletin of Parapsychology* for the publication of experimental work. It appears in connection with a new review, *La Tour Saint Jacques,* edited by M. Robert Amadou.

THE INTERNATIONAL CONFERENCE OF ROYAUMONT

This was held from April 30th to May 4th, 1956, in the old abbey of Royaumont at Asnières-sur-Oise, under the presidency of M. Robert Amadou, with the aid of the Parapsychology Foundation of New York. Its main theme was the relation between psychology and parapsychology, but the programme also touched upon the contacts between parapsychology and psychiatry, ethnology, the history of religion, and psychosomatics. I myself was assigned the task of surveying the attitude of Catholic theology towards psychical research.

Members of this Conference were well-known specialists in various subjects: doctors, psychiatrists, psycho-analysts, anthropologists. Among those who contributed papers were Professor Servadio, editor of the review *Parapsicologia* and Professor de Martino, both of Rome, Professor Zorab of the Hague, Professors Eisenbud and Kahn of New York, Professor Meier of Zürich, Dr Donald West of London (then Research Officer of the Society for Psychical Research), and, from France, Professors Jean Lhermitte of the Academy of Medicine, Delpech of the Faculty of Science at Marseilles, Martiny of the School of Anthropology, and others. This list again shows the scientific quality of the discussions, whose speakers were voluntarily restricted to a small number. It demonstrates the care taken to keep the work on a purely scientific basis. Only one allusion was made to spiritualism—to dismiss it as illusory—and the talks were devoted to extra-sensory perception, the *psi*-factor and the phenomena of levitation.

THE BELGIAN COMMITTEE FOR THE SCIENTIFIC INVESTIGATION OF PHENOMENA REPUTED TO BE PARANORMAL

This dates from 1948. Its official title is *Le Comité Belge Pour l'Investigation Scientifique des Phénoménes Reputés Paranormaux*. Articles of association adopted in May 1949 define its objects thus: "Article 2. The Committee's aim is to study, objectively and scientifically all which emerges or seems to emerge from occultism, whether it be astrology, fortune telling by cards, palmistry, clairvoyance, hypnotism, mediumism, parapsychology, numerology, dowsing, spiritualism or any similar theories or practices, and to bring the results of its researches to the attention of the public, by all possible means."

I am noting here some of the academic distinctions of the members of this association; they are evidence of the undoubted competence of these persons to evaluate paranormal data, especially in connection with dowsing (or radiesthesia) which is one of the main subjects of this investigation.

M. Areno, a Doctor of physics and mathematics, and an astronomer of the Royal Observatory of Belgium.

M. J. Bessemans, a Doctor of medicine and surgery, Professor (and formerly Rector) of the University of Ghent, Professor at the School of Criminology and Scientific Detection.

M. J.-J. Babon, a Doctor of medicine, surgery, and anthropology, with a degree in criminological science, head of the psychiatric clinic at the University of Liège.

M. R. H. Deguent, director of the School of Criminology.

M. M. de Laet, Doctor of medicine and surgery, Secretary of the Ministry of Public and Family Health, Professor of Legal Medicine at the University of Brussels.

M. A. Dorsimont, civil electrical engineer, with qualifications in radio telegraphy.

M. Grosjean, geological engineer, chief mining engineer, head of the Belgian Geological service.

Fr. P. Grosjean, S.J., member of the Society for Psychical Research.

M. P. Levy, a political economist and Professor of Statistics.

M. F. Olbrechts, a Doctor of philosophy and letters, Professor at the University of Ghent.

To these established specialists, trained in the disciplines of philosophy, of the sciences, and of different technologies relevant to the data of psychical research, we must add various conjurers, indispensable for the exposure of tricks which an ordinary scientist might not even suspect.

This committee has exerted a remarkable influence. It has published numerous articles, some in scientific periodicals such as the *Archiva Medica Belga,* or the *Archives Belges de Médécine, Sociale Hygiene Médécine du travail et Médécine Legal* (Belgian archives of social, industrial and legal medicine and hygiene) or *La Revue International de Police Criminelle*) (The International Criminal Police Review); and some in papers intended for the general public, like *Micro-Magazine*. In addition to this, a number of radiophonic lectures have been given as part of the scheme of work of the international radiophonic university.

Occultists, spiritualists, mediums and clairvoyants are firmly excluded from this scientific society; they appear there only as guinea-pigs, objects of study, and they have no voice in the committee which weighs their evidence. We have to acknowledge that they show no eagerness to present themselves in spite of the invitations, the pressing offers, made by this redoubtable tribunal, which has not delayed in establishing a reputation for scepticism and intransigence in occultist circles; these latter cannot, however, accuse it of ignorance.

We shall return to this group when we summarize the current conclusions of psychical research.

In concluding this historical sketch reference should be made to British and American work in Psychical Research. The London Dialectical Society and various individuals, including well-known chemists and physicists, were already studying the subject in the sixties and seventies of the last century. Members of the Ghost Society, founded in 1852 at Cambridge by Edward White Benson, later Archbishop of Canterbury, continued to investigate hauntings and kindred phenomena after leaving the university. One of them, Henry Sidgwick, later took part with Frederic Myers and others in founding the Society for Psychical Research in 1882. The fact that its early members were University men, trained in the disciplines of philosophy and science, probably helped to establish and maintain its extremely high standards. From the beginning it insisted upon "a spirit of exact and unimpassioned enquiry" in the collection, verification and discussion of its data. Its members were not to be held to accept "any particular explanation of the phenomena investigated nor any belief as to the operation in the physical world of any forces other than those recognized by Physical Science". Its aim was "to collect facts while holding no collective opinion about them" and the facts were to concern telepathy, clairvoyance, hypnotism, apparitions, hauntings and "the phenomena commonly called spiritualistic".

One of the Society's first publications, *Phantasms of the Living* (1886), dealt with apparitions of persons about to die, or in serious danger. Three years later it organized the great Census of Apparitions. Sittings with mediums for both physical and mental phenomena were and are undertaken. Poltergeist infestations were investigated, and their frequent connection with the presence of a maladjusted child or adolescent was noted. Experiments in telepathy followed; of the qualitative kind perhaps the most striking were those undertaken by Dr Gilbert Murray between 1910 and 1920, with members of his family and others, and those later undertaken in collaboration with the B.B.C. at various times. Among the quantitative, statistically measurable kind mention should be made of the experiments with electrical apparatus designed by G. N. M. Tyrrell, and of those conducted with Zener cards by Soal and Bateman, which, incidentally, produced evidence of precognition. Other fascinating aspects of the Society's work include the investigation of the "trance personalities" of mediums through word-association tests, the exploration of connections between psychical research, psychiatry and psycho-somatic theory, and the collation of what are called "cross-correspondences" in the automatic writings of a group of persons some of whom had never met.

The Society has always kept in close touch with foreign scientists with similar interests, and has numbered among its presidents Charles Richet, of whose work so much has been written here, and Dr Gardner Murphy, of the American Society.

This latter, founded by William James the philosopher, was at one time united with the English Society, but resumed a separate existence in 1905. It maintains a close and friendly relationship with the English Society.

CHAPTER II

SUBJECT MATTER AND METHODS OF PSYCHICAL RESEARCH

SUBJECT MATTER

Our historical sketch has already enabled us to form some idea of the vast and varied field open to investigation by psychical research. It consists of the extraordinary, in the widest sense of the word; everything, that is, which seems to depart from the ordinary, the normal, the predictable, everything whose existence arouses speculation as to its cause, everything which does not seem completely explicable in terms of the interplay of psychical, chemical, biological or psychological forces as they are known to contemporary science. Thus it will be seen that the subject matter of parapsychology must be that enormous heterogeneous mass of disconcerting incidents which provides a multitude of editors, writers and lecturers with most effective means of attracting and retaining the attention of readers and hearers avid for marvels. Need we enumerate them? They range from the most down-to-earth phenomena to the most ethereal.

There are levitation; the lifting and movement of heavy furniture; "apports" or the transfer of various weighty or fragile objects from place to place; the throwing or falling of projectiles in "haunted houses"; the "bilocation" of human beings (an occurrence usually termed in England "the appearance of a phantasm of the living"); strange raps or bangs heard on walls, tables or other furniture; sympathetic magic; sorcery; the prodigies attributed to yogis; extra-sensory perception; thought reading; "absent-treatment" or suggestion exerted from a distance; radiesthesia or dowsing, with all its different ways of detecting the unknown, from hidden springs to future events; psychometry, or mysterious knowledge drawn from contact with objects belonging to, or used by, some other person; paranormal healing of every sort; all the forms of precognition, astrology with its individual or national horoscopes, clairvoyances, palmistry, fortune-telling by cards or tea leaves, crystal gazing, waking premonitions, "hunches", precognitive dreams; spiritualist phenomena, materializations, transfers of sensation, etc. All these constitute the subject matter to be investigated by specialists in the paranormal.

"Paranormal" is a hard term to define. It presupposes that the boundaries of normality are clearly outlined; but are they? Where does normality cease? Does not the concurrence of completely natural causes sometimes produce phenomena which seem to be extraordinary because they are completely unexpected, even though each of the details of which they are composed has a normal explanation? And what about chance? With its unpredictable caprices, its disconcerting coincidences, it indwells normal life, without needing special explanation. The play of circumstances alone can have very odd effects.

Here is one incident typical of many. During one of my visits to Rome there was a very slight earthquake, so slight as to be hardly perceptible. There were no victims and no damage, except for a single strange incident; a stone ball was loosened from the top of the façade of a church near the Quirinal, and fell accurately on to the head of a German seminary student who was passing by, killing him instantly. There was nothing paranormal about the series of coincidences which ended in this impressive fatality, nor was it the subject of a parapsychological investigation despite the interest and curiosity shown by occultists.

To make sure that a case is paranormal in character, in the first place all possible natural explanations must be exhausted, and in so doing full account must be taken of all the factors (and all their ramifications) which have combined to produce it. It may then prove difficult, in surveying the phenomena lately enumerated, to be absolutely certain that such and such instances were in fact paranormal. This is why psychical research has first of all to begin investigating subjects which only belong to it by hypothesis, because they can only provisionally be considered paranormal. Only at the end of his investigation can the research worker affirm that the case really comes within his terms of reference, and is in actual fact paranormal. Before even being able to analyse those extraordinary occurrences which should apparently be classed among those due to causes as yet unknown, it is essential that the research worker should verify the fact that they have indeed happened. Parapsychology finds itself in the curious position of a science whose very subject matter may not exist. For with regard to each one of the varieties of phenomena just cited, scholars and philosophers are to be found who quite simply deny that they exist at all and refuse point-blank to make them the object of serious scientific study.

The first task of parapsychology must therefore be to attempt firmly to establish the existence of its subject matter as such. We have seen how persistently Charles Richet demanded that this embryo science should devote itself to the critical appraisal of psychical phenomena, so that their authenticity might be guaranteed. This is still, today, the most urgent preoccupation of all parapsychologists and psychical research societies worthy of the name. We shall see how arduous and disappointing this task can be, and what pitfalls beset those who undertake it.

Once the existence of paranormal phenomena is indeed established, parapsychologists will have to tackle a second problem, and investigate whether these phenomena originate in non-human entities (discarnate spirits, angels, demons, God) or whether they should be attributed to what Dr Rhine has called the *psi*-factor, a function of the human soul not yet recognized by official psychology. If this second hypothesis be valid, the paranormal would be no more than a manifestation of a natural faculty still little understood; it should be progressively absorbed into the realm of ordinary psychology as the psyche is more fully explored. In that case parapsychology would be only a provisional stage in the development of psychology itself.

METHODS OF PSYCHICAL RESEARCH

As the most urgent and immediate objective of psychical research is the critical examination of the data put before it, its methods must primarily be those essential to all inquiries as to matters of fact, i.e. observation, the evaluation of evidence, and scientific experiment.

The evaluation of evidence is vital; all the more so since the most characteristic and significant instances usually crop up not simply without being previously arranged, but also quite without warning, and in the presence of witnesses totally unprepared for them. This happens, for example, in spontaneous telepathic communications.

Moreover the strange and often worrying character of such events produces in those who experience or witness them an emotional shock and suggestibility apt to flower all unconsciously into imaginative amplification, and to render objective testimony very difficult.

It is then of the first importance closely to examine each piece of evidence and then to compare them all with one another, in order to remove all the imaginative constructions subconsciously elaborated even by witnesses of the utmost honesty and integrity. We are all incapable of registering a chemically pure perception of fact, unconnected with any extraneous matter accompanying or following our sensations.

Every image we receive is instantaneously associated in the subconscious with a multitude of others which modify, enrich or distort it. No two people see the same thing in exactly the same way. If we ask a number of different witnesses, all in good faith, to describe an incident in which they took part we are certain to find considerable discrepancies in their statements; a fact well known in courts of law. Still more is this the case where moving, worrying, mysterious events are concerned, and a lively emotional reaction is provoked.

I should like to quote here a typical case of such discrepancies as demonstrated by specialists in psychical research. It concerns an experiment carried out during the winter of 1921 in a room of the Metapsychical Institute with the famous M. Pascal Fortuny. This experiment was of capital importance, since it was during the course of this *séance* that M. Fortuny accidentally discovered his gift of clairvoyance which was later the subject of so many examinations and publications. This experiment was reported on the one hand by Dr Eugène Osty (for thirteen years president of the I.M.I.) in his book *Pascal Fortuny* (1926 edition, p. 33); and on the other by M. Jean Chaboseau in his book *La Voyance* ("Clairvoyance") published in 1948 (p. 65).

Dr Osty's Version

Madame Geley took a fan from a table in the room, presented it to Fortuny, and said to him, "Now we shall see if it is all chance. What does contact with this object give you?" Still joking, and with no other motive than to imitate the ways of clairvoyants and also to see just how far chance would favour him, P. F. stroked the fan and cried out, "What is it? I have a feeling of suffocation! And I can hear beside

M. Chaboseau's Version

Surprised by this power, which he had not previously known, M. Pascal Fortuny offered himself for experimental purposes. Dr Geley having silently put a fan in his hand, he declared,

"Thirty-two years old. Tuberculosis. Adèle."

me 'Elisa'!" Madame Geley was stupefied with amazement. This fan had come to her from an old lady who had died seven years before the incident, of congestion of the lungs. During her last illness she had used it to fan herself. The friend who had looked after her was called Elisa.

The fan had belonged to a young woman who had died of consumption at the age of thirty-two. Her last word was the name of her nurse, "Adèle".

It will immediately be understood that if a statement about a paranormal incident is to be of value it must be taken down and put on record directly, in such a way that neither in waking life nor in sleep can the subconscious modify the given original facts which are already and inevitably a little distorted even in the moment of being recorded.

I have myself often found on re-reading a statement written directly after observing an incident or hearing an account of one, that in telling the story afterwards I had, unconsciously and in all good faith, either added something or altered this or that circumstance, so that it no longer corresponded exactly either with the original statement or with the incident itself.

One of the most distorting factors in the observation of events, and one which at once diminishes the value of evidence, is bias in the witness. It is essential, for a really scientific statement, that the person who narrates what he has seen or heard should not be influenced by prejudice, passion, partiality, or feeling of any sort which, all unknown to himself, may modify his powers of perception, and make him believe either that he has seen what he expected or wanted to see, or that he has not seen what has been going on before his eyes because *a priori* he has taken it for granted that no such thing could happen.

It is well known that to wait tensely for something one is expecting, whether it be desired or feared, can create an illusion of seeing or hearing it. This can happen for instance to a man out shooting, who is on the watch for game. A dead leaf blown by the wind, or a moving branch, can make him "see" the animal he is waiting for, "see" it sometimes with extraordinary vividness; yet all those clearly visualized details exist only in his imagination.

At Assisi, at 6.30 p.m. on Shrove Tuesday, February 10th, 1948, two visitors from Perugia declared that they had seen the statue of our Lady on top of the façade of the basilica of St Mary of the Angels swaying. As is well known, enormous crowds from all over Italy and even from other countries maintained that they too could see the statue moving. When the diocesan authorities, after a rigorously scientific investigation (to be described later, for it was exemplary in its objectivity and lack of bias) had established and publicly declared the fact that there had been no movement, no trembling, nothing corresponding to what the masses of pilgrims thought they had seen, gradually they all ceased to notice the motion of the statue.

Had there been anything but collective auto-suggestion? In any case the Catholic hierarchy did not rely upon the sensations of ardent believers. It insisted upon a free and objective scientific inquiry.

Even the sincerity and the complete objectivity of witnesses are not enough to make their evidence watertight. They must bring a trained mind and a spirit of critical detachment to what they see. A trained mind is especially necessary where phenomena of this kind are concerned. When those who saw a flying saucer declared that the object was at such a height, moved at such and such a rate, had such and such measurements, their remarks were received with considerable caution; everyone knows how hard it is to determine without the appropriate instruments the distance of an object whose size is unknown or the size of an object whose distance is unknown.

As well as being able critically to analyse a series of phenomena it is often essential to have had a long experience of similar incidents, and to be very much alive to all the factors which may intervene, all the background circumstances which may affect the results. Thus, when it is asserted that a small round table turns by itself at the mere touch of the sitter's hands, the first thing an experienced witness will do is to make sure that it rocks backward without being pulled by the medium; this is infinitely rarer than seeing it go forward, or rock from right to left and vice versa, movements which anyone can fake with a little sleight of hand.

In a house supposed to be haunted by a poltergeist, the skilled observer knows that the most important thing, on which all else depends, is to watch the starting point of whatever object is displaced. It is the only way to exclude explanations other than the paranormal, the only means to discover what agency set it going. But when witnesses are asked, "Did you see the object begin to move?" they reply almost unanimously that they were not looking when it started on its trajectory, that it emerged from a dark corner or from somewhere behind them or outside their field of vision (why should an invisible spirit hide itself?). The observation instantly loses almost all its significance.

Where phenomena emerge by way of psychological automatism, as in the oscillation or gyration of the dowser's pendulum, the movements of the ouija board, automatic writing and so on, it has been noted that persons whose scientific or philosophical integrity is beyond all doubt have nevertheless not always been able to look at such activities with that detachment which would have shown them the play of subconscious energies escaping from conscious control, and creating the erroneous impression that some entity distinct from the visible human beings present had come upon the scene.

The good faith of the witness, the sincerity of his evidence, his high personal intelligence and the possession of remarkable aptitudes in other branches of science or technology are not enough to guarantee the accuracy or the value of his observations in the field of psychical research. The aptitude needed in this specialized field is built up of many very different components, including a careful training in technique, a sort of clinical *flair* in the psychiatric and psychological side of the work, and a long experience of handling cases. The true explanations are sometimes so unlikely, so hard even to suspect, that one is tempted to dismiss them out of hand as completely fantastic, or unbelievably revolting. We have sometimes had to endure the most stubborn and painful resistance from respectable authorities before, by producing irrefutable proof, we were able to convince them of the unwelcome truth.

In pointing out the dangers to be avoided, we shall note some of the unimaginable trickery practised not only by consciously fraudulent persons but also by the subconscious minds of the completely honest. An ideal psychical research worker should possess a synthesis of talents and a richness of personal experience which it is almost impossible to find in one person. This is why parapsychologists so often prefer to round off and complete their personal observations by scientific experiments.

These consist of attempts to evoke under laboratory conditions the phenomena whose reality one wishes to authenticate and whose nature one wishes to study. The greatest care is taken to reproduce, as far as possible, the background, conditions and circumstances favourable to their appearance and to the ease with which they can be observed. The most suitable witnesses are chosen, and the utmost accuracy is ensured in the use of recording instruments. There is also strict and complete control.

Two methods of experiment in scientific parapsychology have already been worked out and are well known. They are not of course mutually exclusive, and should indeed complement one another, since they correspond to two divergent tendencies of the human mind. They are the quantitative method and the qualitative method.

THE QUALITATIVE METHOD

Those who use this first method set themselves to prepare

and to carry out a pattern experiment, controlled in every detail. The first essential is to compile a complete and exhaustive list of all the factors involved, and then to estimate what part each plays in achieving or varying the result obtained. It is easy to see that such experiments as these necessitate a great deal of preparatory work, done without hurry and without preconceived ideas; they also demand repeated alteration, adjustment and reorientation carried out with all the patience given to laboratory experiments in chemistry, physics or biology.

The International Metapsychical Institute has worked out techniques of this kind, perfecting conditions for experiments in telepathy and clairvoyance; as the *Association Française d'Etudes Métapsychiques* (French Association for Parapsychological Studies) has done in connection with telekinesis by means of the apparatus already mentioned for testing the flow of drops of water.

One objection always persists: how can we be certain that there is not some imponderable factor, at present unrecognized, which has intervened to distort our interpretation of the experiment? On the other hand, it is surely reasonable to consider the possibility that chance may have been at work —for instance in a telepathic experiment—and may have contributed to the apparently perfect result of a single test.

It is the duty of the research worker always to bear in mind these misleading factors, and to attempt to exclude them from his calculations.

THE QUANTITATIVE METHOD

To eliminate these tenuous possibilities of illusion, the mathematically minded have recourse to quantitative methods. Their aim is so to multiply experiments of a given kind that the proportion of successes achieved cannot possibly be explained in terms of chance. It should thus be possible, if not to *explain* a parapsychological event, at any rate to have an absolute proof of its occurrence, which is in itself a valuable scientific achievement. The mathematical laws arising from the calculus of probability put it out of the question that more than a certain definite proportion of successes can be attributed to chance. The greater the number of experiments the more certain are the conclusions to be drawn from their results.

The value of quantitative experimentation in physics, engineering, chemistry, biology, etc., needs no demonstration. In these spheres statistics have a very large part to play, and one which is universally recognized. Where statistical calculations have been worked out on a large enough scale it is possible to reach solid conclusions, upon which valid deductions can be based, and effective action be taken. Such methods are used, for instance, to assess metal stresses, the knowledge of which is essential for engineering work, the building of bridges, etc., and also for calculating the complexity with which biological characteristics are transmitted through generations of fruit-fly.

Does this all hold good in the realm of psychology? Is it possible to set out in mathematical terms realities of which each is differentiated from the rest by those elusive features, and real though indefinable variations, which philosophers call notes of individuation and which made the wisdom of the ancients declare that *Omnium individuum ineffabile*; every individual is inexpressible, unique. Where health is concerned, even physical reactions vary so much that doctors have recognized the soundness of the saying, "There are no illnesses, there are only sick persons". Psychological reactions, conscious or subconscious, are more diverse and unpredictable still. There are no two faces exactly alike, no two handwritings which are identical in the eyes of a graphologist.

This diversity among human beings is such that if we observe a complete identity of reactions and expressions between two of them we are immediately certain that they are in touch with one another. If an examiner who has to correct thousands of papers for the great French examination, the *baccalauréat*, finds two alike, whether in French composition or in the philosophical thesis, he does not hesitate for one moment before deciding that the two candidates have "collaborated".

In the realm of psychology, indeed, complete rigidity is impossible. Every feeling, every image, every idea is connected with a living individual interplay of associated imagery, conscious or subconscious, which cannot be found in identical form in any two human beings. In psychology one cannot well argue from a given number of cases since in the eyes of the psychologist no two cases are ever quite the same. Only exterior events, tangible and measurable results, can be alike; every psychological mechanism must differ from every other by inexpressible and incalculable shades.

What then can statistics be worth to the practising psychiatrist, whose knowledge is not academic but is worked out in close, almost intuitive, contact with human lives as they are lived; that is to say, in ceaseless flux and change, not neatly dissected for appraisal. Must not the same label be used to cover what are in fact realities as diversified as a collection of appendixes at a surgical exhibition? It is impossible not to think of all the infinite variations in degrees of responsibility, and conscious control, not to mention the play of free will which may affect spontaneous reflexes, instinctive reactions, and the association of images.

It is therefore necessary to make reservations and to be extremely circumspect about the usefulness of quantitative methods. If the results are positive (for instance in an experiment in extra-sensory perception) inasmuch as the successes notably surpass the chance average, it is plain sailing. We have clearly to deal with results which cannot be explained in terms of chance; and we are confronted with the need for a scientific explanation of their origin. But if the results are inconclusive because the number of successes corresponds with the chance average, what is to be deduced? I think that in a certain number of cases one is not justified in concluding that the experiment was of no significance.

For critical purposes, we describe and examine an experiment organized by the C.B.I.S.P.R.P., the Belgian Committee for the Scientific Investigation of Reputedly Paranormal Phenomena, to which we referred in the previous chapter. The experiment was so organized as to achieve results which could be assessed in terms of the quantitative method, and compared with chance averages as worked out in accordance with the calculus of probability.

M. Paul Lévy, a Professor at the Belgian Institute of Higher Studies, and a member of the Statistical Council, gives an account of this test of radiesthesia in a pamphlet published in 1953 and entitled, "An experiment in the use of radiesthesia for tracing missing persons" (*Une Experience radiesthesique de recherche des disparus*).

(The practice of radiesthesia is, by the way, an extension of what is traditionally known in England as dowsing, or water-divining. The dowser searches for underground water, by walking across the land to be explored holding a forked hazel twig in his hands. It is said that when he passes over the hidden spring or stream the twig twists violently, apparently of its own momentum. This technique as such has been used in the search for other minerals. A curious development of it, better known on the Continent than in England, is for the dowser, now known as a "radiesthetist", to use a pendulum or a ring suspended from a thread, which he passes over a large-scale map; it is said to oscillate over the spot where underground water lies. This method has also been employed in France, of late years, for police purposes, in trying to trace the bodies of the drowned; and also in medical diagnosis, where the pendulum, moved across the patient, oscillates over the site of his disease. Before the development of the practice of breeding chicks whose colour is sex-linked, so that cockerels can be weeded out directly they are hatched, the Japanese used to diagnose the sex of eggs in this way; the pendulum was supposed to move in a clockwise circle for males, and widdershins for females, and the practice was carried on on a commercial scale. It is also sometimes applied with accuracy to pregnant women, but not, so far, on a large enough scale for statistical evaluation. *Translator's note.*)

We can summarize the forty-four pages of this pamphlet. On March 3rd, 1952, the Belgian Committee appealed to dowsers of all nations to cooperate in an experiment which might make it possible scientifically to determine, by statistical methods, the efficacy of radiesthesia in discovering (a) whether a missing person were still alive and (b) his whereabouts, alive or dead. Precautionary measures of all kinds were taken to prevent trickery, fraud and leakage, and also to ensure that no traps were set for those taking part, and that nothing should be done to disturb the setting of their work, to mislead them or to vitiate their findings.

For each inquiry those who took part in the experiment were given a photograph less than five years old of the missing person together with an autograph specimen of his handwriting. Each worker had ten sets of these documents to study, and ten answers to supply. The actual facts about each case were sent in sealed envelopes to an official of the committee before the trial experiments began.[1] The radiesthetists had thirty days in which to complete their work. The results were to be examined in the presence of an official who was to draw up a report on them, and the Committee pledged itself to publish the main points of this report.

All the documents, photographs and handwriting alike, were authentic, and the utmost care had been taken to prevent any occurrence that might have modified their usefulness from the radiesthetic point of view. The experiment was admirably mounted.

To the question, is the person dead or alive, 300 replies were given. It is obvious that if the replies were simply based on chance, as in a game of heads and tails, the proportion of correct replies would be fifty per cent, and the number, in this instance would be 150.

[1] This meant of course that the Committee should have considered the possibilities of telepathy with those who supplied these facts, or of precognition of the result of opening the envelopes, in explaining any positive results of the experiment. [*Trans.*]

In point of fact there were 152 correct replies and 148 mistakes. But the crude results were broken down into considerable detail, and it was established that the percentage of correct replies concerning the living was higher than that concerning the dead: 53·9 per cent as against 43·2 per cent. Mathematical experts, however, by calculations which need not be reproduced here, concluded that no statistical significance inhered even in the larger number of successes attained in gauging the number of the living, which lay well within the range covered by the chance average.

With the question of localizing the missing person, dead or alive, the chances of success were very small, since the place to be pin-pointed might be any town in the world. The Committee received no more than 142 replies to this question, of which only 24 gave the correct countries involved, and among these twenty named Belgium. In accordance with the quantitative method, assessed in terms of the calculus of probability, the results of the experiment were declared to be inconclusive.

This verdict does not satisfy the psychologist, who must ask: can one possibly add the case of a dowser living in the Indre-et-Loire department, and working on data concerning a remote town in almost any country (documents came from Germany, England, South Africa, the United States, and Switzerland, among others) with that of a Belgian dowser working, unknown to himself, on Belgian data originating close by? Again, can one properly include in a list of items whose overall total shows poor results the case of Madame G., who gave seven out of ten correct answers to the question of whether the missing person were alive or dead, and one correct country out of ten (while every country in the world might have been the right one, and every city in each one of them)?

Those who organized the whole experiment realized however that they would have to take into account certain considerations which led them outside the purely mathematical field; for instance in connection with research-worker A, who correctly assigned to Brussels the person for whom he was looking, research-worker G, who indicated the Mathurin district of Paris instead of the Molitor district, research-worker D, who gave Chantilly for Senlis, and finally research-worker W, who located his quarry south of Thonon instead of Nyon. Such successes as these certainly raise questions which need answering. The Belgian Committee cancelled them out, by setting off against these surprising results the erroneous replies given by the same research workers. Mathematically speaking, this was quite correct.

All the same, from a psychological point of view it was remarkable that someone living at Vesinet, near Paris, with the whole surface of our planet to choose from should succeed in locating south of Thonon a person who was in fact at Nyon, twenty kilometres off as the crow flies; that another, at Gosselies in Belgium, should indicate Chantilly instead of Senlis, nine kilometres distant; and that yet another, in the Indre-et-Loire district should reply Paris, Molitor tube station instead of Paris, rue des Mathurins. Even if these workers gave other replies which were completely wrong it seems to me that these successes raise a doubt that cannot be ruled out by the hypothesis of chance. The mind is not set at ease by such an explanation, and seeks further data.

Though the quantitative method is reliable when it shows positive results, clearly corroborated by probability, it is less useful, as the above remarks will show, when its results are negative. The number of failures registered in such instances cannot cancel out a success duly verified and proved. I should like to associate myself whole-heartedly with Fr de Tonquédec's assertion in his recent book, *Merveilleux métapsychique et Miracle chrétien*, 1955 ("*Psi*-phenomena and Christian Miracles"): "A phenomenon which is vague and cannot be repeated may nevertheless have characteristics so well-attested, so numerous and so significant that it is impossible to explain it in terms of chance."

DANGERS TO BE AVOIDED

If parapsychology still needs to demonstrate the reality of its subject matter, the paranormal, this is because those who seek to establish its existence are always meeting obstacles which do not arise in the physical sciences, where exactitude is easier, but belong to the order of psychology or even psychiatry. To chart the hidden reefs which may wreck the results of long and patient research and of many series of observations and experiments, the parapsychologist needs to know, not as a matter of academic science, but through personal experience, a certain number of distorting factors, which can generally be detected only by a special flair and skill.

The study of one of these dangers will show, if it is still necessary to do so, the complexity and the exceptional risks of psychical research.

PSYCHOLOGICAL AUTOMATISM

One of the first snags awaiting the parapsychologist is the fact that psychological automatism can give the impression that some outside entity is at work. We have already had occasion to refer to the subconscious mind, that extraordinary and impenetrable "other-self" which hides all those activities, recognized and unrecognized, which go on, or are carried on, within us all the time, waking or sleeping; activities which escape more or less completely from the control of the everyday self.

These activities are infinitely numerous, and infinitely varied. They continue incessantly within us; sometimes in the form of perceptions which, though not consciously recognized, etch themselves permanently into the memory,[1] sometimes in the form of associations of images or ideas which spring up (without reference to the desire or control exercised by the ordinary self) through a sort of automatic process which can be wonderfully logical, but which can also be strange or even

[1] As in "subliminal advertising". [*Trans.*]

chaotic. These associations, happily or absurdly juxtaposed, do on occasion emerge into the upper levels of the mind, which can then either drive them back whence they came, or make some conscious use of them.

Generally, in the waking state, the incessant workings of the subconscious mind are crowded out of our knowledge, to remain unrecognized, even though through a multitude of reflex-actions and associations of imagery they subserve all conscious activity, internal and external; or, at any rate, exert a considerable influence upon it. In the state of sleep, on the other hand, the subconscious functions freely and spontaneously in the dreams which it never ceases to create, or in nervous or reflex movements quite unknown to the controlling self which is temporarily cut off from the rest of the human organism.

Between these two extremes, conscious waking life and sleep, there are certain intermediary states in which a kind of psychological dissociation occurs and the subconscious invades the province of the conscious mind, without the latter's knowledge. The Self, otherwise engaged, absorbed perhaps in some emotional state, is preoccupied and distracted, and gives a free rein to the subconscious. States of tension on the one hand, or relaxation on the other, bring about a sort of trance condition favourable to the incursions of the Other Self; incursions which we know as daydreams, fancies, involuntary reflections, released by a kind of automatic process to which the Self remains more or less alien. When it realizes what is going on, it becomes clearly aware of this sort of duplication of itself, and sometimes recognizes the fact in such very significant phrases as "I wasn't quite there", "I was in the moon", or "I had a fit of absent-mindedness", "It escaped me", "How could I have done that?" "I wasn't myself", "I can't see myself doing that".

Such an automatism is at work where people "doodle" words or drawings on a wall or the flyleaf of a book while they carry on an absorbing telephone conversation; it was this, again, that made Pasteur drink the glass of water in which he had so carefully washed his grapes to get rid of the germs on them.

In parapsychology this automatism will show itself in the trance state by a true psychological dissociation which will make the muscles act independently of all conscious control under the direction of the subliminal self which, superseding the conscious mind, gives to the subject himself and to all who see him the impression, more, the certainty, that a strange being has invaded his personality. This very often happens with the insane. It can however equally well occur in well-balanced people, as I have explained at some length in analysing experiments with the ouija board, with "talking glasses" and with automatic writing, in Chapter Six of my book *Peut-on Communiquer avec les Morts?* (" Can we Communicate with the Dead?")

The patient is of course convinced that he has nothing to do with the movements he undergoes, and declares in complete good faith that he feels himself to be impelled by an outside force. Does not the Other Self take in our dreams the shape of strangers whom we see and hear although they are no more than our own creations?[1]

It is obvious that the psychical research worker must be very much alive to the possibility that psychological duplication of the kind just sketched may be at work, especially when he is dealing with cases of radiesthesia, table-turning, etc., in which unconscious automatism plays so large a part. Fr Athanasius Kircher, S.J., in his treatise *Magnes Sive de Arte Magnetica* ("The Magnet or on the Magnetic Art") published in Cologne in 1643, was already maintaining that the movements of the divining rod were caused by the unconscious muscular actions of the dowser.

Pierre Janet worked for a long while on the multiple mani-

[1] Readers familiar with the work of Jung, which is not very well known in France, will accept this statement with reserve, remembering his fruitful hypothesis as to archetypes common to a universal unconscious. [*Trans.*]

festations of this psychological automatism, manifestations which had mistakenly been thought paranormal; and he shed much light upon them. He maintained in *L'automatisme psychologique* ("Psychological automatism"), Part II, Chapter III, that "we have brought together three kinds of activity, which are certainly analogous: the use of the divining rod, the use of the pendulum, and thought-reading"; the movements of the rod and the pendulum being simply the automatic, unconscious exteriorization of perceptions or at any rate of internal imagery, operating below the level of consciousness.

ILLUSIONS AND HALLUCINATIONS

It is unnecessary to give more than a bare indication of these obstacles constantly encountered in psychical research. Where the extraordinary is involved, the human mind and senses are peculiarly prone to exaggeration and the construction of elaborate fantasies. Even the most stable and critical persons are not always proof against the suggestive power inherent in a set of circumstances whose vividness is heightened by fear, by longing or simply by tension, all of which form favourable soil for the growth of hallucination, individual or collective. This danger is too obvious for us to linger over.

POST-DATED DISTORTIONS OF PERCEPTION

Even when the greatest possible objectivity has been maintained in the recording of all the stages and details of an apparently paranormal event, the parapsychologist must still beware of distortions made after the occurrence by the subconscious mind. For the impressions made upon us by even the most accurate perceptions do not remain inert and immobile in the memory; they are frequently recalled, and every time this happens the subconscious modifies them a little, telescoping one series of incidents, linking others with associated imagery, tidying everything up in a way which, without our realizing it, may seriously distort the original picture.

The narrative which, soon after the event, was perfectly in accordance with the record made by our senses, is little by little embellished with various adornments, given new shades of meaning, generally enriched; certain features are effaced or cut down, others are reinforced or newly created by the imagination, and without an idea of what we are at, we risk altering the original story, sometimes to a quite fantastic degree. We can also fall victims to distortions arising in dreams which may, unknown to us, link themselves to the real memory of what happened.

In order to defend oneself against these unsuspected sources of falsification it is therefore necessary to write down an account of the paranormal event as soon as possible after its occurrence; or, better still, if this can be done, to record it while it is still going on, by ciné camera and tape recorder. How many times have film and play-back restored the knowledge of what really happened, re-established the truth distorted by the workings of the subconscious in honest witnesses, who, faced with an accurate mechanical record of what took place, recognize, not without amazement, their involuntary embroideries.

We must therefore be extremely suspicious of evidence collected several months or even years after the paranormal event. Its accuracy, whatever the sincerity of the witness, must be extremely doubtful.

THE MORALS OF HYSTERIA

We now approach a submerged rock much more dangerous, and much better hidden, than the preceding ones. The realm of the paranormal is the earthly paradise of hysterical persons. The parapsychologist must be able to discover them and get rid of them.

It is well known that, in medical parlance, it is practically impossible to define the word hysteria. Many eminent specialists have recognized this, and have ceased to use it. Babinski declared, "It would be a good thing if the term hysteria could be abandoned, for, taken in its etymological sense, it does not correspond to any of the symptoms we have in mind."

Fr de Sinety, S.J., in his excellent book *Psychopathologie et Direction* ("Psychopathology and Spiritual Direction") declares (p. 145): "In a word, every possible type of character, in all its varying aspects, exists among hysterics as among other women,[1] and, if one wishes to study the character of hysterics as such, without prejudice or preconceived ideas, one is forced to the conclusion that it is impossible to give any typical character at all."

We shall not attempt to deal here with the physical and medical aspect of hysteria, with its repeated crises, and its protean physiological and pathological manifestations, simply because they are classified as typical of the condition.

The word hysteria is currently used to indicate a very special kind of psychological or moral deviation; a capacity for more or less conscious pretence, or for totally unconscious deception, which destroys all faith in the evidence, the attitude or the actions of these patients, of whom one can cheerfully say that lying comes as naturally to them as breathing. Scientifically, it would be preferable to give up the term hysteria, and to indicate the condition by such words as pythiaty, mythomania, unconscious romancing.

The term used is not important; what matters, and what should be kept in mind, is the very special nature of this falsification. In its origin, we shall find a powerful invasion of the unconscious and the subconscious, bringing their irrational forces constantly to bear upon the conscious and willed activities of the normal Self, to such a degree that the patient may suffer from complete dissociation, and a secondary personality may come into play.

Above all, we observe a raging egocentricity, with an

[1] In English the term is applicable to either sex. [*Trans.*]

intensification of feelings, emotions and passions and a sort of irresistible craving to make oneself interesting, to attract attention, to be talked about; to be blamed and condemned just as much as to be admired and praised.

What must be noted before all else—and what is too often forgotten by too many observers of the extraordinary—is that deception, as practised by the hysteric, does not arise from the wish to cheat others in order to exploit them, but solely from the need to attract notice; this variety of neurotic longs for people to discuss her. We must also note another characteristic feature of hysterical self-dramatization, that the creation of the romance, the saga, the imaginary play, is in no way the fruit of a conscious and deliberate effort of composition. All the work is carried on in the subconscious. But the result is put forward to psychological consciousness with so much life and colour and detail and plausibility that the patient herself is drawn into it, and finishes by really believing in the reality of what the Other Self has brought into being. At certain moments she is genuinely convinced of having seen, heard or done all that her imagination has created, and she is persuaded that she is in truth the interesting, illustrious, heroic or tragic person whose part she acts.

This conviction can become so intense that the hysteric is capable of swearing false oaths, even upon the Crucifix or the Blessed Sacrament, to prove her lies are true; she will go quite calmly to Communion afterwards without confession. We have seen some who, after having deliberately deceived their confessor about some grave sin, then received the holy Eucharist from him with touching piety.

This same conviction makes the hysteric capable of exposing herself to severe punishment, as if she were really guilty of all the sometimes abominable things of which she accuses herself. She will accept with impressive remorse the most humiliating and difficult ways of making up for her imaginary faults, above all if these penances are sensational enough.

It is easy to see from all this that observers whose own make-up is simple and normal, and whose moral conscience is honest and straightforward, will find it difficult to be forearmed against frauds of this nature, let alone to detect them. The simplicity and ease with which they will swallow all that is said and done by the hysteric is equalled only by their anger, their excessive harshness, leading to the imposition of pitiless and unjust penalties, when they have at last discovered for themselves, or have been forced to recognize, the gross deceptions practised by these sick people.

Is not hysteria the real origin of many famous and puzzling historical occurrences such as the terrible trials of witches, fiercely accusing themselves, with many confirmatory details, of having gone to the Sabbat, or such as most false visions and false miracles? In the face of so-called paranormal phenomena the first question always to be asked is whether hysterical mythomania has any part to play in them; this is very often difficult and uncomfortable to track down, but to do so saves a great deal of subsequent fruitless investigation, and prevents painful confusion among those observing the case. In many instances the advice of an expert on handwriting may be enough to reveal characteristic symptoms. It is impossible sufficiently to stress the fact that this diseased psychological dissociation, which can give the impression of play-acting of the most revolting kind, does not mean that the sick person is incapable of frankness and moral integrity in so far as her conscious actions are concerned. On the other hand, even though a person may be proved to have all the virtues, tried and true, she may also suffer from hysterical self-dramatization.

Perhaps some evidence will be useful here. First of all there is that given by Dr du Poray Madeyski, the psychiatrist attached to the Sacred Congregation of Rites, who was sent by Rome to conduct a scientific inquiry into the case of Teresa Neumann. In his famous book, which unfortunately does not appeal to a very wide public, since it is written in medical and psychiatric terms (*Thérèse Neumann de Konnersreuth*, Paris, 1940) he quite definitely confirms the diagnosis that this celebrated invalid suffers from hysteria. But he adds this tribute

(p. 292): "The existence of hysteria in Teresa Neumann does not in any way diminish her moral stature, her personal dignity, her sincerity, her piety, nor even the possibility of her holiness; it does not diminish the merit of her pious intentions or of her virtuous life."

It is for this reason that when the Bishop of Ratisbon declared on December 10th, 1937, "In the present state of affairs, the authorities of the Church decline to take any responsibility as to the reality of the so-called absolute fast, and the other phenomena of Konnersreuth", he did not exclude the possibility that Teresa might have true virtue.

Father P. Siwek, S.J., in *The Riddle of Konnersreuth, a Psychological and Religious Study* (New York, 1953, Dublin 1954), with the imprimatur of Cardinal Spellman, a book which is the most accurate and best documented study of the Konnersreuth stigmatic so far published, clearly brings out the fact that though the Hierarchy has the gravest doubts about the genuineness of the marvels attributed to Teresa, these doubts do not exclude the possibility "of solid Christian virtues and genuine mystical states".

Dr Biot and Dr Galimard, in a book published in 1955 and entitled *Medical Guide to Vocations*,[1] write in a similar way: "Even the most extraordinary hysterical manifestations and dramatizations are not the same thing as conscious deception (this is in fact extremely rare) but arise from the unconscious imitation of a state of mind violently desired" (p. 100). "It is thus that lying can blend inextricably with piety and with a life of true renunciation. . . . A high degree of spirituality and even of real sanctity can be accompanied by manifestations of hysteria." Perhaps I may be allowed to cite here two cases of unconscious mythomania particularly useful in showing what great difficulties can be encountered in investigating the authenticity of paranormal phenomena.

First of all, a case of mythomania in the realm of religious prodigies which I had to look into myself at the request of a religious body. It concerned someone who seemed to have

[1] London, Burns and Oates; Westminster, Md, Newman Press.

had no other food than holy Communion for a whole year, and who had been kept under such control conditions that fraud seemed inconceivable. She was bedridden, day and night, in a French hospital caring for some 200 patients. Her room was on the second floor in a corridor whose entry door was locked every evening. The kitchen was in the basement; this too was locked all night, as was the larder leading out of it. To reach the latter, therefore, no fewer than three keys were needed.

After two months of this pretended total fast, modified only by daily Communion, the person alleged, in order further to disarm suspicion, that she had no bowel movements. Faced with this anomaly the doctor in charge, after consulting a professor in the faculty of medicine, made an artificial opening, so that she might have an intestinal lavage from time to time. They relied of course on the allegations of the patient, whose good faith seemed obvious. Only at the end of a year of this presumed total abeyance of the functions of eating and elimination did the nun in charge of the kitchen find a fragment of a key in the larder lock. A discreet inquiry elicited the fact that it came from the housekeeper's bunch of keys, which were only taken off at night. She slept in the same room as the "patient" and every night put her bunch of keys down on a chair between their two beds. A trap was set at once, and suspicion was confirmed. The faster, drawn out of her subconscious state, had to make a clean breast of what had happened. She had never ceased to feed herself at night, thanks to the housekeeper's bunch of keys, and had no hesitation in communicating every morning.

The circumstantial evidence had seemed to make it plain that no additional controls were necessary; it was clearly apparent that the person could not nourish herself secretly; her good faith had seemed so complete both to the almoner who was her confessor and to the doctors to whom she alleged that she had no evacuations, that no one could possibly doubt the reality of the extraordinary fact, that nothing had been eaten for a whole year. What case of *inedia* could have seemed better established?

The second case of hysterical mythomania occurred in a hospital in the Paris district. A patient eluded the watchfulness of doctors and nurses again for a whole year by making strange inexplicable abscesses, with the aid of subcutaneous injections of one or two drops of turpentine. Microscopic analyses, naturally enough, showed no microbial infection, and the liquid burnt the tissues of the dermis and formed little by little strange lesions of the epidermis which intrigued the medical profession and made the mysterious case extremely interesting. The anxiety of the doctors, and the admiring visits of the clergy struck by the resignation and the edifying words of this victim of a strange and persistent illness, satisfied the need to attract attention in this unsuspected hysteric. The prolongation of her stay in hospital, where she lived at other people's expense, could not seem other than agreeable to her.

At my first visit after discovering signs of self-dramatization, I advised a detailed search which brought about the discovery of a small syringe and a bottle of turpentine carefully hidden at the back of a drawer. How could a doctor without experience of the tricks of hysteria have suspected that she had been inflicting such absurd injuries on herself for a whole year, with the sole object of becoming a centre of interest?

We have even more reason for extreme prudence when we encounter those who live by marvels and pseudo-marvels; yogis, clairvoyants of all temperaments, and mediums, all people who use resounding publicity methods to advertise themselves as magicians out of the common run. Exhibitionists of this sort are easily recruited from amongst hysterics of both sexes.

Charles Richet said *a propos* of mediums, "Let us repeat that they have a right to all our respect, but also that they call for all our distrust"; this formula is also applicable to hysterical patients.

FRAUD AND CHEATING

The subconscious mind is not the only source of faked paranormal phenomena. It is not indeed exceptional to meet people who deliberately and consciously exploit the credulity of the public and the open-mindedness of experts by claiming that they bring about or endure such things. The methods they employ are extremely varied and improve with the progress of modern techniques.

Among these frauds are some who can no longer deceive any but the stupid and the wilfully credulous; they do not interest psychical research workers, who know them all too well. We shall not stop to enumerate their standardized tricks, many of which are described in books of conjuring, and also in a work published in 1952 by M. Robert Tocquet, of the International Metapsychical Institute, *Tout l'occultisme devoilé* ("Occultism Exposed").

But apart from ingenious tricks such as these, with their high entertainment value, there are some of which even experienced parapsychologists must beware, since they are intended deliberately to mislead them, and may invalidate the results of experiments planned on the most critical lines. These are the expedients employed by mediums, clairvoyants, psychometrists and even certain radiesthetists, in order to obtain spectacular results.

Some are quite simply organized frauds, in which "specialists" pass on confidential information to one another, and collaborate in various other ways. M. Robert Tocquet exposed a number of these practices, which ruined and brought into ridicule a series of experiments dealing with extra-sensory perception.

Others are devices based on physics or chemistry which research workers have detected in the hands of various yogis and mediums. There are obvious ones, like the use of the electro-magnet, or of a magnetized ring or bracelet, or of those filaments or ribbons of nylon which, invisible in a dim light, are excellent means of "magical" levitation. Others are less easily exposed, like the employment of phosphorescent substances emanating from the mouth or skin of the medium, or of phosphorized gauze, which gives the illusion of extremely photogenic ectoplasm. Lastly, among the rarest and most up-to-date bits of apparatus there is the tiny wireless set made in the United States—and still very expensive, though extremely profitable—the transmitter of which is placed at the base of the agent's pharynx, while the receiver is hidden in the percipient's hair; thus producing the most staggering results in experiments in thought transmission. There are a number of laboratories in the United States which specialize very successfully in the manufacture of such instruments of fraud.

SWINDLING AND DELIBERATE DECEIT

Sometimes impudent lying is combined with trickery in the attempt to make certain individuals into star performers; in cases of this kind, parapsychologists have to be especially careful not to be victimized, and have their reputation ruined in the process.

There was, for instance, the case of the notorious Peter Hurkos the radar-man, the soothsayer, of whom the French Press was so full in 1951 and 1952. He claimed to have seen in a bush a lock of hair and a shred of clothing belonging to the little girl Joelle Ringot, whose murder at Phalempin had stirred public opinion very deeply. Unfortunately for him, it was some hundreds of yards away from the place where the child was found; she had been killed near her home, and hidden on the spot, in a cesspool. Before this discovery, French papers and reviews had described, with a profusion of detail, just how Peter Hurkos had been called in by Scotland Yard, and had, thanks to his remarkable gift of clairvoyance, brought about the recovery of the Stone of Scone (stolen in 1951 from Westminster Abbey) and had given the police the names of the guilty persons.

Alas, two shattering denials exposed this wonderful soothsayer. First of all the Assistant Commissioner of the Metropolitan Police wrote (March 2nd, 1951) to Professor Bessemans, of the Belgian Committee for the Scientific Investigation of Reputedly Paranormal Phenomena: (Hurkos) "came to this country at his own expense and was given the chance to exercise his powers in discovering the Stone; but his efforts produced nothing that could help the police".

The other denial came from Mr. Chuter Ede, then Home Secretary, who, speaking in the House of Commons on February 23rd, 1951, said: "The gentleman in question whose activities have been publicized (though not by the police) was among a number of persons authorized to come to Westminster Abbey to examine the scene of the crime. He was not invited by the police, his expenses have not been refunded by the Government, and he did not obtain any result whatever."

These official denials antedated by several months the stories about Hurkos' discovery of the Coronation Stone which appeared in the French Press. French newspapers omitted to publish them.

It is certainly neither easy nor pleasant, when some "paranormal" occurrence has once been written up in the Press, to acknowledge trickery or fraud that has come to light too late. After putting forward in all good faith the claims of a fraudulent medium, a "visionary" who is a pathological liar, a faked stigmatic or a bogus child-wonder it takes exceptional courage, rare integrity, publicly to own that one has been deceived and fooled. A man of no more than average courage and integrity may simply let things slide, allow the deceit to continue, or even use all his ingenuity to keep the false report in circulation as long as possible. During all this time parapsychologists may be basing plausible hypotheses on the supposed facts.

La Revue métapsychique for July 1955 published with considerable tact and with praiseworthy frankness a case of fraud which had long been known but kept secret, first by Dr Geley and then by Dr Osty who succeeded him as President of the

International Metapsychical Institute. Here it is: Mr Lambert had published in the S.P.R. Journal for November 1954 (Volume 37, No. 682) a critical account of Dr Geley's reports on the experimental work conducted for some years at the International Metapsychical Institute with the medium Eva, who specialized in materializations. In September 1927, having learned that Dr Osty had found among Dr Geley's notes some photographs showing that one of Eva's materializations was a fake, a fake achieved with the help of Madame B., who had taken part in the I.M.I. *séances*, he questioned Dr Osty about the whole subject. The latter, after some hesitation and under a pledge of secrecy, showed Mr Lambert some photographs which, seen under a stereoscope, showed that the "materialization" was attached to Eva's elaborately-dressed hair; he acknowledged that "this was a ridiculous fraud". In Mr Lambert's own words, "Osty also told me that he wanted to publish his discovery. As, however, Richet and Schrenk-Notzing protested energetically against it, and M. Jean Meyer, a militant spiritualist who financed the Institut Métapsychique, also forcibly demanded the concealment of the scandal, Osty had to give up the idea of publishing his discovery."

To form any objective judgement of the attitude adopted by the directors of the I.M.I. it must be remembered that a great deal of public interest had been aroused, over several years, by numerous publications, illustrated by photographs, issued by Dr Geley, Dr Schrenk-Notzing and others, on the subject of Eva. Mr Lambert added: "Now that twenty-five years have passed since Osty showed me the stereoscopic pictures . . . there appears to be no reason for further secrecy. I have therefore thought it my duty to report Geley's suppression of highly suspicious details from his published work."

La Revue métapsychique frankly comments (p. 54): "The facts related by Mr Lambert are substantially correct, and no one need scruple to acknowledge them." After having given certain considerations which soften a little the unfavourable view taken of Dr Geley, and which explain why Professor

Richet decided to keep silence about this more than probable piece of fraud, the *Revue* concludes thus: "However detached one may be (and this is not always easy) is it not always more satisfying to note some curious new fact than not to note anything at all? Unhappy incidents such as this should move us less to criticize others than to keep a strict watch over ourselves."

On this final remark this chapter on the aim and methods of psychical research must end. Aim and methods alike call for extreme prudence, constant distrust, and a watchful and critical frame of mind. In the realm of the paranormal it is important to keep one's feet on the ground and to work rationally, without yielding to imagination or emotion, and least of all to passion.

This means that we should rigidly exclude from psychical research work all those who are temperamentally impressionable, suggestible or neurotic, although such people are quite especially attracted to this kind of investigation. At best it will exhaust them, at worst it may make them completely unbalanced.

At the same time we should banish from scientific groups devoted to these studies all who are dominated by passionate preconceptions, or victims of blinding prejudice, incapable of considering coolly and objectively the facts before them.

Only on such conditions as these can parapsychology succeed in establishing on a solid basis the existence of paranormal phenomena, in order to discover their philosophical, scientific or religious explanation.

CHAPTER III

PSYCHICAL RESEARCH AND RELIGION: TWO CLEARLY DEMARCATED FIELDS

Before examining the problem of any possible conflict between psychical research and religion it is necessary clearly to distinguish between psychical research itself, defined as the critical scientific study of paranormal phenomena with a view to establishing their existence and their nature, and a sort of metapsychology which is, in fact, a system of religion or philosophy, such as spiritualism or occultism. Adherents of such systems do not usually adopt a scientific attitude or use scientific methods of searching for objective truth; they are apt to behave in a partisan fashion, seeking to find in the facts at their disposal the confirmation or illustration of their teachings which are based not on experimental proof but on so-called revelations or messages attributed to higher beings or discarnate spirits.

We have seen already how much harm has been done to genuine psychical research by these ardent enthusiasts, who have attempted to use it to further their own theories, or whose main concern has been to obstruct all such critical work as might eliminate the necessity for elaborate occultist systems, or lay bare the emptiness of spiritualist phenomena.

With these distinctions in mind, let us see in what ways psychical research and religion can come into contact, colliding or cooperating with one another.

As far as basic theory is concerned, if each of these questing activities of the human spirit were confined to its own field, they would have no occasion to meet. The religious point of view is on a different plane from that of parapsychology. Miracles spring from causes far above those natural forces which belong to the sphere of the latter. Doubtless psychical research will, and should, on occasion examine paranormal phenomena whose ultimate cause is supernatural; but it cannot reach or detect the supernatural as such, since this is beyond its competence.

In a work written in 1954, *Merveilleux métapsychique et miracle chrétien* ("*Psi*-phenomena and Christian Miracles") Fr de Tonquédec set himself to throw light on the contrast between these two sets of apparently similar phenomena. Among his most significant remarks are (p. 65): "Parapsychological phenomena are derived from natural causes and circumstances, physical, physiological or psychological, and therefore bear the mark of determinism"; and again "Parapsychology as a whole remains within the realm of determinism, while Christian miracle springs from beyond this realm in spontaneous obedience to the liberty of its author, God."

Despite the supernatural appearance borne in certain cases by psychical phenomena they remain by definition part of the natural order. It can therefore be postulated that parapsychology can have no more occasion to come into conflict with religion than do medicine or psychiatry, astronomy or palaeontology. While these disciplines remain in their own field without touching on questions of faith or morals they cannot be opposed to religion.[1] Science as such studies no

[1] It is only honest, surely, to recognize that the difficulty lies precisely in delimiting the frontiers of each discipline. It is for instance useless and wrong to gloss over the fact that however mistaken Galileo may have been in his theological ideas, where astronomy was in question his views were more accurate than those of the theologians who condemned him. Their respective fields had not been distinguished. [*Trans.*]

more than data and their causes or antecedents in the order of nature. If an occurrence is supernatural in origin, science can establish that it has happened and analyse the circumstances which precede and accompany it; but it cannot discover the ultimate explanation, which lies outside its terms of reference.

Psychical research works of integrity themselves recognize this; let us quote only one of them, M. Robert Amadou, the former editor of *La Revue métapsychique,* and author of *La Parapsychologie*. After having asserted on p. 321 of his book that "parapsychology gives more embarrassment than support to spiritualism", he adds "and as for that vital principle itself, to which some attribute the *psi*-function, what has it in common with the image of God, created for eternal beatitude?"[1]

In parapsychology (p. 322) "there is nothing that can shed any light for us on the soul and its survival, the soul and its immortality. For the immortal soul, the divine spark within us, is neither the dwelling place nor the cause of parapsychological phenomena"; (p. 293) "We have to dissect something sacred when we adopt the attitude of psychical research. But the sacred which can be dissected is not genuinely sacred. Let us thank psychical research for effecting a necessary purification."

Psychical research cannot therefore rule out the possibility of intervention by forces outside the natural order, without trespassing beyond its own field, and losing competence and authority alike. It can and should however put this question on one side, while it attempts to establish the reality of the phenomena submitted for analysis, and to find an explanation valid in terms of man's natural faculties, normal or supernormal. Psychical research as an experimental science does not have to take into account either miraculous agencies or the normal and religious circumstances of any given phenomenon, and is not concerned with any religious or philosophi-

[1] This is a rather schizophrenic distinction. Whatever "the vital principle" may be, it is clearly part of the entire human being; and the entire human being is created to that end. [*Trans.*]

cal theories put forward to explain the occurrence of that phenomenon.

In acting thus, it adopts an attitude like that of the *Bureau des Constatations médicales de Lourdes,* of which more will be said presently. In this committee, recruited only from doctors—of whom over 1,500 pass through Lourdes every year—there can be no question of miracles, only of paranormal cures which cannot be explained scientifically. Every doctor is admitted whatever his religious convictions or materialist opinions, or even his morality. The only things to be considered are his medical qualifications and his specialized knowledge.

The committee makes no inquiry whatsoever into the religious circumstances which may have accompanied or preceded the cures submitted to it. This medical body has to set aside all religious and political considerations, and concentrate solely on the following three questions:

1. Was this person ill? What was the exact diagnosis of his condition?
2. Is this person in fact cured?
3. Does this cure go beyond the processes of nature as we know them?

If the three answers are in the affirmative, the committee cannot of itself decide that the cure is miraculous; that is not its business. It must, in such a case, send the medical dossier on to a higher commission, composed of scientists and theologians, sitting in Paris; this body alone is competent to investigate the religious background and circumstances of the case, and to decide for or against the possibility of a miracle. Its conclusions are then submitted to the bishop of the diocese to which the patient belongs. Only he is authorized to make the final decision.

In this way the Bureau works, like the parapsychologist, on the purely natural and scientific level, without touching in any way on the part that supernatural agencies may have played in paranormal healing.

Where trustworthy and conscientious psychical research workers are concerned we should avoid imitating the attitude of certain timorous and wavering Lourdes pilgrims who will hesitate to bring some apparently miraculous cure to the attention of the *Bureau des Constatations* lest that committee of doctors should deny, or at the very least abstain from recognizing, the supernatural character of that cure. A true faith in the miraculous has no fear of an objective critical study of a supposed miracle where it is entrusted to men of intellectual integrity, free from the prejudices and preoccupations of the partisan materialist scientists of the nineteenth century.

True miracle has nothing to fear from true science.

Although it is true to say that religion has nothing to fear from parapsychology one cannot be so categorical about parapsychologists, for these are not only minds in search of truth, but men, complex human beings, full of different tendencies, opinions, prejudices, passions, men who tackle parapsychological problems with a whole host of preconceived ideas which, even if repressed into the subconscious by a genuine wish for objectivity, remain active and capable of distorting the data received.

It must be said that the overwhelming majority of those who have devoted themselves to psychical research have in France been either spiritualists or materialists. Their partisan anti-religious attitude did not fail to influence their work and to show itself in a certain unseasonable aggressiveness not always sufficiently held in check by their more objective colleagues. It has already been noted that M. Jean Meyer, who financed the first French centres for psychical research, was a "militant spiritualist" who exercised a most unfortunate influence on the general trend of their investigations and publications.

M. Charles Richet was not a religious man. A destructive agnosticism pervaded his approach to all religious concepts, and his scepticism with regard to the possibility of divine intervention was obvious. He put Christian and pagan miracles on the same plane. It seemed to him that, once all that sprang from simplicity and credulity had been obviated, what remained was a matter of *psi*, that little explored function of the human organism.

Of Joan of Arc he wrote: "Her voices and her visions were perceived by no one else, so that it must be admitted that they were subjective. It would be an over-simplification to suppose that they were ordinary hallucinations, for these hallucinations were followed by too many hard facts and duly verified predictions to be dismissed as the delirium of a madwoman. . . . One can hardly doubt that Joan was inspired. It is best to admit, as a probability, without drawing any conclusions, that Joan of Arc had certain psychic powers." But the case of the saint is cited between those of analogous paranormal phenomena associated with Cicero, Tacitus and Brutus on the one hand, and instances of the divination evinced by sleepwalkers, of haunted houses, and table-turning, on the other.

As for the cures at Lourdes, after quoting some of the most remarkable such as those of De Rudder, and Gargam, Charles Richet concludes, "even if these case records are accurate, they cannot be said to prove the existence of a new parapsychological force. All they show is that the central nervous system possesses, under certain conditions, a new and altogether extraordinary power over organic phenomena." The assumption that there can be no possibility of supernatural intervention is extremely striking.

Nearer to our own time J. B. Rhine, who exercises a considerable influence among contemporary psychical research workers, has no scruple in trespassing into the spiritual sphere as a destroyer of all the most essential values of religion. In his book *The New World of the Mind* (translated into French under the misleading title *Le Nouveau Monde de l'Esprit* which in itself suggests that he has gone beyond the frontiers of parapsychology), after alluding to "an unprogressive religious leadership", he adds (p. 201): ". . . to these central questions even the scholarly leadership in all the religious systems simply does not have answers that would satisfy the ordinary standards of evidence of everyday life. . . . In the face of that realization dogmatic religion comes to assume the shape and proportion of a gigantic group delusion, shutting itself off deliberately from the tests of reality by which its position could be verified, and by which its course towards greater positive knowledge would be directed. For in this old attitude is an almost complete abandonment of realism, a surrender to a system of unverified fantasy that in a single isolated individual would be characterized as psychotic."

Of "the unverified authority of ancient manuscripts" (presumably the Bible) he declares: "What magic spell has kept us all stymied so long in religion? What enchantment keeps the world charting formulas that may be rubbish for all it knows?"

Even belief in an afterlife is ridiculed: "Religious ethics have for ages and for many peoples of the world been oriented towards a life beyond the grave. . . . Yet no orthodox Church organization has ever undertaken to get the matter of a future life investigated scientifically, as other problems have been. . . ." Let us stop there; it is enough to justify Fr de Tonquédec's criticism: "We are faced here with the most opaque intellectualism, and in professing it Rhine is not so far as he believes from the materialism against which he struggles with praiseworthy zeal throughout his book."[1]

[1] A number of other points should also be made clear. First, that the French translation of the book, as quoted by Fr Réginald-Omez, is a good deal more anti-religious than the original American text. Second, that in their context the passages cited bear a different connotation from that which they carry as set in isolation here. Thus, in its setting, the paragraph about "a life beyond the grave" could not by any stretch of imagination be thought to "ridicule belief" in that idea. Third, that in "the Churches" to which Dr Rhine is accustomed, one or another of the highly Protestant sects of America, Luther's traditional condemnation of "the harlot Reason" in favour of an obscurantist emotionalism is still followed, and that for Fundamentalists to doubt the literal inspiration of the Bible as it stands (not as it is interpreted by the living authority of the Church) is anathema. The final point, and it is vitally important in a world

Finally, it is well known that Mrs. Eileen Garrett, President of the Parapsychology Foundation, who originated and directed the International Conference for Parapsychological Studies at Utrecht in 1953 was for a time involved in the Spiritualist movement, some of whose idioms are still retained in her book *My Life as a Medium*, although she has long since left it and adopted an almost completely neutral frame of mind towards the nature of her powers and what they reveal.

These few examples are enough to illustrate the necessary distinction between parapsychology (or psychical research) and parapsychologists (or psychical research workers) before

---

which can increasingly talk and think only in the idiom of science, is that, as was maintained as far back as the time of St Thomas Aquinas, there are not two incompatible truths, theological and secular. Truth is one; and all that is must ultimately be integrated into that single whole. Truth is one, in however many languages it may be expressed; and it surely cannot be considered irreverent for men to explore, discuss and define what they have discovered in their own terms if these are the only ones intelligible to them. It must be remembered that theological expressions have so often been distorted and misused over centuries of religious controversy that to the majority of mankind they no longer succeed in conveying their original meaning. The axiom that the scientist must not multiply hypotheses must also be borne in mind. Without this indeed it is hard to see how what is due to the natural though little understood activity of the *psi*-function could be separated even in theory from the miraculous, the direct action of God. It should be plain, moreover, that God can act indirectly through *psi*, as through any other created thing. *Psi* is indeed often highly developed as a by-product of contemplation; and there seems no reason to suppose that this was not the case with St Joan, although Richet's remarks are so indignantly dismissed. Bearing all this in mind it seems rather hard to condemn Dr Rhine as anti-religious simply because he finds incomprehensible the ecclesiastical terms he has come across, and wishes to use his own methods and idiom in the attempt to establish the existence alike of *psi*, of a life beyond the grave, and of God himself. *The Times Literary Supplement* reviewing *The New World of the Mind*, in October 1948, noted that it was "written to refute the materialist conception of human personality". The bitter Communist attacks on the works and conclusions of Dr Rhine seem to prove that it has been successful in so doing; this is hardly an anti-religious feat. [*Trans.*]

setting out to consider the relationship between this science and religion.

It is of course possible to name psychical research workers untouched by any hostility to religion; witness the following lines by M. Robert Amadou (*La Parapsychologie,* p. 334): "One merit of parapsychology is that it simultaneously protects us against superstition of various kinds and convinces us that the holy, the mysterious and the supernatural cannot be explained away in terms of their lesser reflections, that shadow is not substance, and that neither man nor the world is God." And again: "This young scientific discipline holds, and will continue to hold, the key to understanding many phenomena. It does not, and it will not ever show that everything in the universe and in man is wholly explicable in terms of the exact sciences."

THE CATHOLIC CHURCH AND PARAPSYCHOLOGY

The Catholic Church; this expression could denote the supreme Authority of the Church, of the single Head of this spiritual family, acting as such and committing the whole Church by his official word. It should be noted at once that the Catholic hierarchy as a whole has never adopted, either in acts or definitions binding upon the faithful, any special position with regard to psychical research.

The dogmatic pronouncements of the supreme ecclesiastical authority of Rome are indeed very much fewer than is commonly believed alike by Catholics and non-Catholics. They are reserved for defining the essential truths of religion; the dogmas imposed in the Catholic Faith do not proliferate.

But the phrase "the Catholic Church" can also indicate expressions of thought on the part of members of the Catholic hierarchy, expressions of thought which do not involve the supreme Authority of the Church. This may be because they are only concerned with disciplinary order (such as, for instance, many of the measures taken by the Holy Office, which can forbid the general reading of a book without necessarily taking up any definite position about it from the point of view of the Faith); or because they come from subsidiary authorities, and are limited to such and such a diocese, or groups of dioceses, or because they reflect no more than theological opinion, whether it be personal, or that of a group, or even that of all theologians.

We are, then, no longer in the presence of any teaching to which the Church is officially and definitely committed; but we face a general opinion which, though it does not demand the assent of the faithful, and may indeed develop further, is nevertheless authorized and has the right to be considered as representing the general trend of thought in the Catholic Church.

It is in this last sense that the phrase "the Catholic Church" will be used here.

The Church has always been extremely cautious about marvellous occurrences connected with religion. Those wonders which, arousing general curiosity and damping down all sense of critical objectivity, release floods of mass-emotion, are greeted among responsible authorities in the Church with a lively distrust, and come up against a marked desire for strict scientific investigation.

Rome has intervened much more often to condemn false miracles, illuminism, false apparitions and so on than to guarantee the authenticity of supernatural phenomena, whose genuineness is never in point of fact made a matter of faith.

For the Catholic Church bases its faith on such solid causes of belief, on such an accumulation of reasoned proofs that it does not worry in the least about new sensory manifestations which could be further adduced in its favour.

Furthermore, it has already on record so many instances of supernatural interventions on its behalf which have already been checked and established that it has the right to be detached and critical towards such new instances of the marvellous as have not been strictly examined and checked.

Catholic religious faith is based upon the essential relationship between man and God as Creator and Redeemer, and on the doctrinal revelations of the Old and the New Testaments, not on material wonders which, although impressive, add nothing to the riches of doctrine and act only on sensibility, imagination or emotionalism.

For these reasons the Catholic Church has long set about discovering and establishing on a solid basis criteria which facilitate the distinction between purely natural events, or more or less conscious mystifications, and phenomena whose origin is really supernatural.

It did not wait for the birth of parapsychology in the nineteenth century to embark on critical research work designed to establish the reality of paranormal phenomena, and to discover possible natural explanations for them.

CRITERIA OF THE CATHOLIC CHURCH FOR INVESTIGATING MARVELS

As early as the seventeenth century Benedict XIV published his famous decrees on the Beatification and Canonization of Servants of God, in which he set out the rules to be followed in assessing the reality of miraculous cures, visions, apparitions, etc.

In 1751 Fr Azevedo, S.J., of the Congregation of Rites, drew up, at the request of the same Pope, a very large volume in which he made a doctrinal synthesis of all these decrees.[1]

The shortness of this volume makes it impossible to quote this work at the length that it deserves. It is extraordinarily well informed about all the difficulties which may arise in trying to establish the authenticity of a true miracle. I should like to cite the criteria which he enumerates for the investigation of miraculous cures (Book IV, Part 1, Chapter 8, p. 223 of the 1841 edition):

For a true miracle it is required:

That the disease should be serious and incurable, or at the very least difficult to cure.

[1] *Benedictae Papae XIV doctrina de Servorum Dei Beatificatione et Beatorum Canonizatione in synopsim* redacta ab Emm. de Azevedo S.J. Sacrorum Rituum Consultore. 1751.

That it should not have developed to the stage when it might normally have cleared up.

That medicines capable of explaining the cure should not have been used.

That the cure should be sudden and complete: that it should have "a moral, though not necessarily a mathematical instantaneousness" (*sic*) (p. 225). The author comments that in certain cases a period of from three to ten days does not exclude "moral instantaneousness" which remains relative to the time normally needed for a natural cure.

That the cure should not have been preceded by a notable "evacuation" or "crisis" capable of bringing it about naturally.

That the disease should not recur some time later.

These criteria of Benedict XIV are still valid, and show an enlightened care to distinguish between the true and the falsely marvellous. Why are they not applied to cases of paranormal healing today?[1]

Note also the following interesting exposition of the powers of the imagination written two hundred years ago: it uses the terms of the medical science of its time but it is remarkable for its prevision of what is now known about the power of autosuggestion and of the action of the subconscious in bringing about apparently miraculous cures.

(P. 279) "The imagination is capable of engendering Distempers and of causing them to vanish; of provoking purgings and vomitings which may restore Health. It can diminish for a space the degree of Pain that is felt. . . . Imagination can be efficacious in the restoration of Health, not all in a Moment but little by little, since it acts upon the Humours and Spirits of the Body, which contribute much to the Conquest of the Sickness." The author quotes here the case of Alfonso of Aragon, who was cured as the result of reading, and that of a soldier cured by a violent explosion of

[1] The Society for Psychical Research recently conducted an investigation of paranormal healing on these lines in England. [*Trans.*]

gunpowder, and draws attention to the fact that in such cases the cure may be immediate. He assures the reader that arthritis (presumably psychosomatic rheumatism) can be cured by the imagination. And he adds, "When the Distemper does not proceed from a simple Movement of the Spirits [in modern parlance 'is not purely functional'] but arises because some part of the Body is injured, dried up and immobilized [say 'an organic illness'] then the Pure [nuda] Imagination can do Nothing" (p. 280).

Let us add to these all too short extracts concerning the investigation of miraculous cures the following very relevant remarks about visions and apparitions:

(P. 201) "Visions and apparitions are common to the good and to the wicked. . . . They are graces *Gratis Datae*, which can therefore be given even to sinners. . . . As these visions and apparitions can only be vouched for by him to whom they have been accorded, he does not merit that anyone should have confidence in him over so secret a matter unless he be above all suspicion and rich in heroic virtues. . . . For this reason no vision or apparition should be adduced in causes for beatification and canonization unless it has already been shown that heroic virtue existed and that the end of the subject's life was dazzling in its sanctity."

All this makes it easy to understand the reserve and the severity of the Church towards new visions and apparitions. The current Code of Canon Law indicts "books and printed matter of all sorts telling of new apparitions, revelations, prophecies, miracles . . . unless published in conformity with canonical regulations, which insist that the approval of the ecclesiastical censors must previously have been obtained."

The Catholic Church today has in no way tempered this strictness. Is it necessary to recall the well-known warning issued by Mgr Ottaviani, then Assessor of the Holy Office, and now Cardinal Pro-Secretary of that same Congregation set up for the defence of the Faith of which the Supreme Pontiff himself is the Prefect? This warning was published first in the *Osservatore Romano*.[1] There we read: "Fifty years ago who would have believed that the Church today would have to put her children, and even her priests, on their guard against stories of visions, false miracles and of those so-called preternatural occurrences which from one country to another, from one continent to another, everywhere indeed, attract excited crowds. . . . We have for years been in the presence of a revival of a popular passion for the marvellous, even in matters of religion. Crowds of the faithful assemble in places where apparitions or miracles are supposed to have happened; but at the same time they desert their churches, the Sacraments, the hearing of sermons. . . . The Church certainly does not wish to hush up the wonders wrought by God. She only desires the faithful to distinguish clearly between what comes from God and what does not come from God and may come from our adversary who is also His. The Church is the enemy of false miracles."

COMMISSIONS OF INQUIRY

Inspired by this extreme caution, and in order to disentangle the false from the true, and to recognize and proclaim true miracles the Church has set up commissions of specialists whose duty it is to carry out as ably and critically as possible the most exhaustive and stringent investigations of happenings put forward as miraculous.

The *Bureau des Constatations Médicales de Lourdes* was set up in 1884; but the Church did not wait until that date before submitting the miracles of the Grotto to scientific inquiry. As early as 1858, the very year in which the miraculous spring spurted out, the religious authorities had an analysis made of the water of Massabielle in order to make sure that it contained no element which could account for the cures in a natural way. In addition, a committee of doctors was at once set up to conduct a critical examination

[1] And subsequently in most leading Catholic periodicals in the English language, e.g. *The Tablet, Commonweal,* etc. [*Trans.*]

of the first cures. Only after these had been scientifically confirmed did Mgr Laurence, Bishop of Tarbes, sanction belief in the apparitions of Lourdes. I give the exact words of the official text of approval, for it bears witness to the extreme circumspection with which the Church acts on the subject of apparitions.

This document is dated January 18th, 1862. "In view of the favourable account presented to us by the Commission charged with reporting on the apparition of the grotto of Lourdes and on the events connected with it; in view of the written evidence of the doctors, which we have consulted on the subject of the numerous cures obtained after using the water of the grotto; considering primarily that the effect of the apparition seen (whether upon the young girl who reported it or whether, above all, in the extraordinary results it has produced) could not be explained except by the intervention of a supernatural cause . . . we judge that this apparition bears all the marks of truth, and that the faithful are on solid ground in believing it real. We authorize in our diocese the cult of Our Lady of Lourdes."

The probable miracles have in fact been very numerous. Canon M. G. Bertin counted 3,962 from 1858 to 1917, but official recognition has since the beginning been rarer and more difficult. In fact, from 1858 to the beginning of 1956 only 52 cases have been recognized as miraculous by canonical judgement and by the authority of the bishop. This is because the *Bureau des Constatations* examines with the utmost vigilance each one of the cases submitted to it, in order to rule out all which seem doubtful or capable of a natural explanation.

Professor François Leuret, who was in charge of the work of this commission until his death on May 8th, 1954, said in the course of the Conversations of Saint-Paul-de-Vence (Paris I.M.I., 1955, p. 380): It is "a medical organization whose aim is to be as scientific as possible, an organization accustomed to the examination and verification of the evidence set before it. The part it plays is purely objective. It is not qualified to interpret this evidence; only the theological commissions have the authority to do that and to say whether such and such an established fact is or is not of a miraculous character. The Medical Bureau of Lourdes never speaks of miracles, only of cures."

This Bureau, to which cases are referred in the first instance, sits at Lourdes, and is open to any doctor who goes there. In 1954, 1,541 doctors from twenty-two nations went there and were able freely to join in the discussions and to examine the archives. During the course of the sessions each could obtain case-histories, analyses and evidence of every sort that he might think useful. The Commission has the use of first-class medical apparatus, including a Philips machine for radiography, with the most up-to-date equipment.

Excluding cases of neurosis, which are ruled out at once, every person who claims to have been granted a cure is given a preliminary examination, dealing with his physical condition and with the medical dossier which he should have brought with him, or which has been compiled at Lourdes before the cure. This first examination is carried out by one or two specialists and is followed by another conducted by the whole Bureau at a special sitting convened for the purpose. At the end of this special sitting at which any and every doctor in Lourdes can be present, a written account of the proceedings is drawn up. It gives the answers, signed by all the doctors, to the following questions:

1. Did the disease described in the certificate or certificates exist at the time of the pilgrimage to Lourdes? What were its distinctive symptoms?
2. Was the course of the disease instantly arrested while it showed no tendency to improve? What morbid symptoms then disappeared?
3. Is this a real cure? What certain evidence can be given? Did it take place with or without medical treatment?
4. Should judgement be suspended?
5. Is it possible to give a medical explanation of this cure? Does it fit into the category of natural law?

The Bureau then calls upon the person cured to undergo a second examination the following year. During the interval inquiries are made among the doctors who have treated the patient and the hospitals or clinics which have cared for him, in order to collect a dossier, as complete as possible, of records showing the origin and course of the disease, evidence of the original diagnosis, and of course, the permanence of the complete cure.

If the person cured does not return at the end of a year, or if any of these indispensable pieces of evidence is missing, the case is rejected. Otherwise the Commission undertakes another critical investigation of the whole case. If all the conditions are positive, the complete dossier is sent to a superior Commission situated in Paris, composed of scientists and theologians, who take up the whole investigation once more, adding a moral and spiritual examination of the religious circumstances of the cure.

If this Commission reaches conclusions confirming the judgement of the Bureau of Lourdes it transmits them to the bishop of the diocese to which the person cured belongs. In his turn, and with the help of a diocesan committee set up for the purpose, the bishop studies the case, and if he thinks fit proclaims the cure miraculous; only after this proclamation is the Press authorized to publish the miracle.

I have written at some length on all this, for it shows how extremely careful the Catholic Church is to rule out all apparent marvels for which no scientific and spiritual proof can be adduced. If only such methods could be imitated by all those parapsychologists who are so often tempted hastily to conclude that phenomena are paranormal!

A recent incident admirably illustrates the objectivity of this Commission set up by the religious authorities.

In October 1954 Georges Rouquier made in Lourdes a film *Lourdes and its Miracles* which was shown all over France. Now this film showed first of all someone very seriously ill, stretched out on his bed of pain among other patients, and then the same person, presenting himself, cured, at the

Medical Bureau. The film and the press gave considerable publicity to this gripping "cinematic proof" for the reality of miracles, and to the general release of pictures of a sitting of the Bureau. The diagnosis of the disease, established in the medical dossier brought by the patient, indicated that it was a brain tumour which had for many years resulted in violent headache, severe derangement of the motor nervous system and a complete inability to walk.

In October 1955 the person cured, now in perfect health, returned to the Bureau for the routine second examination. I was present at this meeting in which some forty doctors took part. During the previous year's inquiry an unsuccessful attempt had been made to find an electroencephalogram made before the cure, which proved that the symptoms of serious disease had indeed an organic origin. In view of the fact that this document was still missing, the Commission quite simply disallowed the claim to miraculous healing. There was not a word about the film, the press or public opinion: these considerations do not exist for the Medical Bureau of Lourdes.

Since the Bureau was founded, 1,200 cases accepted the first year have been ruled out after the more thorough examination twelve months later.

MIRACLES AND THE SACRED CONGREGATION OF RITES

We ought to outline here the scientific methods used by the Sacred Congregation of Rites in studying the miracles cited in connection with the beatification or canonization of Servants of God who have died in the odour of sanctity. It was for this Congregation that Benedict XIV worked out those criteria for the judgement of apparently preternatural cures which have already been discussed.

A commission of doctors and specialists has been established to carry out this critical research work. I am sorry not to have space to quote in these all too short pages the very long and detailed questionnaire drawn up in order to detect all those factors which might affect the marvellous and supernatural character of the "miracles" in question.

If only an equally strict verification were demanded for cures attributed to "healers" of every kind, radiesthetists, Christian Scientists, yogis and so on!

AN INQUIRY AT ASSISI

In the spring of 1948, there appeared in the press remarkable stories about a marvel that was happening at the Franciscan basilica of St Mary of the Angels, at Assisi.

In 1932, a statue of the Madonna in gilded bronze over twenty-four feet high, and weighing more than seven tons, was erected at the top of the façade.

At 6.30 p.m. on Shrove Tuesday, February 10th, 1948, two men from Perugia, Messrs Santovecchi and Marocchini, perceived that the statue seemed to be rocking, balancing itself as if it were being carried in men's arms, or as if the chest expanded in a sort of breathing. Hearing of this the local inhabitants rushed to the spot and experienced the same impression. The news spread rapidly, and large crowds assembled from all over Italy.

The religious authorities did not commit themselves to any opinion, but decided at once to undertake a scientific inquiry to test the objective reality of the phenomenon.

First of all the mathematicians and engineers of Assisi attached motion indicators to various parts of the statue to assess its stability. There was no evidence of any movement. They then made observations through telescopes trained from different angles upon the statue; it did not move. Seismographs were suspended inside the statue from a pendulum nearly ten feet long; but, though the spectators outside observed the swaying of the Virgin no seismogram was traced within. Spirit levels were installed inside the statue; not a quiver did they show. A photo-electric cell and an electrometer were used to rule out all possibility that the impression of movement might arise from some variation in the brightness of the lamps surrounding the statue; no such variation in the intensity of their light was revealed.

Someone then had the idea of putting up cameras with telephotographic lenses at various points in the square around the basilica and taking a number of photographs on the same film to see if the pictures covered one another exactly, or showed any overlapping or blurring due to movement; but the outlines were completely clear cut. Another hypothesis was envisaged; that radiations of some sort were emitted by the earth, but very delicate instruments recorded nothing of the kind. There was no escaping the scientific conclusion that the statue remained completely motionless. It followed that the vision of the Virgin's movement corresponded to nothing outside the minds of the onlookers.

The religious authorities tried an experiment as a counter-check; the professors of physics at the diocesan seminaries of Fano and Assisi attempted to reproduce the conditions under which the phenomenon had been seen by placing a statuette in the middle of a circle of little lamps as evening fell. Sure enough they observed just such an apparent swaying as that of the Virgin's statue.

Is it possible to imagine greater care than this to establish objective truth or the use of more critical and exhaustive methods to discover the natural explanation of an apparently marvellous phenomenon?

A CRITICAL INQUIRY INTO THE CASE OF TERESA NEUMANN

The press, which pounces so avidly upon marvels true or, above all, false, was very careful to say nothing about this inquiry or the conclusions drawn from it by the religious authorities.

It took place on Maundy Thursday, 1928, and the following day. The commission of inquiry comprised six distinguished men, Mgr Buchberger, Bishop of Ratisbon, Mgr Kierl, a suffragan Bishop, and four well-known doctors, Professor Killermann, Professor Hilgenreiner, Professor Stockl and Professor Martini, director of the medical clinic of Bonn University.

The diocesan authorities had definitely decided to arrange that the development of stigmatization and the Good Friday ecstasy should be watched under controlled conditions by the scientists. Opposition on the part of the Neumann family prevented the Commissioners exercising the continual vigilance which was essential, and discovering the exact nature of the process thanks to which blood spread across the patient's hands or chest at the very moment when no one was looking. But the conclusion reached in Dr Martini's official report was categorical; the members of the Commission had never seen blood spurting or oozing from the tissues. Bleeding never occurred except when Teresa was hidden under the bedclothes, or when every single witness had been compelled to leave the room, sometimes on the pretext of decency because of a call of nature, and sometimes because it was argued that the heat and the bad air would be too much for Teresa if even one of them remained.

The diagnosis reached by the four professors only confirmed that already pronounced by the medical experts who had visited her on February 27th, 1920, before her ecstasies: "very serious hysteria with blindness and partial paralysis". This second time it was formulated as follows: "a state of serious hysteria, with all the symptoms typical of the disease, including the usual factor of simulation". In spite of the family resistance which hampered this episcopal and medical inquiry, it was concluded that no real stigmatization existed.

In his *Mystiques et Faux Mystiques* ("Mystics and False Mystics"), Paris, 1953, Professor Jean Lhermitte of the Academy of Medicine concludes sadly: "So ends the story of Teresa Neumann. A major hysteric with the deceptive streak that accompanies severe neurosis; it is thus that the stigmatic of Konnersreuth reveals herself to us."

Dr de Poray Madeyski, the doctor attached to the Sacred

Congregation of Rites, maintains the same thing in his book on Teresa Neumann published in 1940 with the Imprimatur of Mgr Traglia, vice-gerent of the diocese of Rome, and with the approval of that eminent jurist, Fr Creusen, S.J.

The Church is the enemy of false miracles even if they arouse a great movement of faith and piety in the world. She works that truth may be known and prevail.

Unfortunately, commissions of control, diocesan or Roman, are not always accorded such facilities as are available at the Lourdes Medical Bureau, where people are entirely at the doctors' disposal for examinations and inquiries. It has just been noted that the opposition of the Neumann family prevented any exact verification of the stigmatization and the total fast claimed on behalf of Teresa, in spite of the guarantee of good faith implied by the presence of the bishop. Professor Leuret, the President of the Lourdes Bureau, when working outside Lourdes has himself encountered complete resistance when he wished to check up on such and such a case of "assured stigmatization", which had been widely discussed.

In cases like these the silence of the religious hierarchy should not be construed as tacit approval. It has not always, either in theory or in practice, the means of verifying the marvellous occurrences retailed by the press with so many varied and contradictory details. Sometimes the secular arm is needed.

Ought we to recapitulate the case of the parish priest who had visions of the "Virgin of the poor tunnel", and, suspended by his bishop, was to be turned out of his presbytery by force, on June 26th, 1948, when a crowd of enthusiasts took his part against the police sent by the local authority at the bishop's request?

The Catholic Church is just as reserved and cautious on the subject of paranormal events attributed to the intervention of the devil. It certainly believes in the latter's existence and activity, but it recommends to its priests the wisest and most careful discernment in judging phenomena presented to them as the work of the spirit of evil, and gives them exact criteria by which to recognize that work.

It should be enough to cite here the most authoritative testimony which could be quoted today, that of Fr de Tonquédec, S.J., who has analysed the origins, nervous or mental, of much of the phenomena mistakenly thought diabolical. It is the fruit of over forty years of experience as an exorcist in Paris, consulted in point of fact, by people from all over France. His book, *Les Maladies nerveuses ou mentales et Manifestations diaboliques* ("Nervous or Mental Diseases and Diabolical Manifestations") appeared with a laudatory letter from Cardinal Verdier:

(P. 12) "While admitting that cases of possession really occur, the Church refuses to put them on record without investigation. If the stories of possession set out in the inspired books, and notably in the Gospels and the Acts of the Apostles, are part of the faith of believers, this does not hold good of those recounted in other books, even if they be the work of saints or doctors of the Church. In the same way, our judgement and interpretation of contemporary occurrences which we may witness remain entirely free. The Church has never used its authority to compel the faithful to believe that in any case of this kind there was true possession." Moreover the Church expressly invites careful critical examination of stories of possession and of current happenings which could be interpreted in that sense. The first thing it recommends to the exorcist is caution. "First of all, before everything else, he should not easily believe in possession" (Roman Ritual of Exorcism). "If then, the preternatural signs indicating the presence of the evil spirit are lacking, the priest should refuse to believe in it."

"It is all too easy—as happens sometimes—to attack as scepticism or as rationalist prejudice the care taken to prevent confusion and mistakes about this point. Ignorance and credulity are very harmful here, and could have serious consequences both for the faithful and their mental balance and for the good name of the Church" (p. 19).

Such is the true attitude of the Church towards diabolical marvels. Events have shown over and over again how well-founded this attitude is. Very many people have been brought to us, even by priests or nuns, as victims of diabolical activity or of black magic, when a little circumspection would have been enough to show that the case was purely psychological, and a little fatherly suggestion, or a course of treatment, would be much more efficacious than any amount of exorcisms, blessings or medals.

THE ATTITUDE OF THE CHURCH TOWARDS NON-RELIGIOUS MARVELS

Directly the phenomena under consideration do not seem, however strange they may be, to bear the stamp of a religious or a diabolical origin, the Church refrains from intervening in a province not its own. This, for instance, is the case at the present moment with regard to the phenomena of radiesthesia, thought reading, telepathy, psychometry and so on, when these occur in a purely secular context.

In 1936 Pius XI encouraged the radiesthetists who had presented him with the collected volumes of the *Bulletin des Amis de la Radiesthesia* ("Bulletin of the Friends of Radiesthesia") by asking Mgr Tisserant, pro-prefect of the Vatican Library, to write to them thus: "I should have written to you much sooner if I had not waited to have an audience with the Supreme Pontiff, to explain to him personally the nature of the researches to which the members of your Association devote themselves, and to tell His Holiness of your wish to receive the Apostolic Blessing for the directors and the work of the Association. The Holy Father was much touched by the feelings expressed in your letter, and has asked me to send you his fatherly blessing. I will add that in order to be able to examine its contents at leisure, the Sovereign Pontiff has kept back the last number of the Bulletin. . . . We shall have the greatest pleasure in being kept in touch with the developments of your work."

On the other hand, in order to correct the abuses committed by certain priests who, under cover of radiesthesia, were practising medicine, which they are not allowed to do, the Holy Office on March 26th, 1942, published a decree forbidding priests and members of religious orders to practise radiesthesia unless their objectives were purely scientific and their experiments completely impersonal. They might not undertake research work connected with medical diagnosis or treatment, the discovery of missing persons, the assessment of character or moral state, etc.; but could practise dowsing for water or metallic ore.

Neither the encouragement nor the disciplinary measures implied that the Church was taking up any definite position in these spheres; they are outside its field.

THE CHURCH AND PSYCHICAL RESEARCH

The Church has no cause to intervene in the purely scientific domain of studies in the paranormal, so long as those engaged in them remain on their own ground. The true Faith has nothing to fear from true Science; for Christians, revelation and human science both spring from the same divine thought, and cannot therefore contradict one another. Apparent opposition can come only from some scientific error which should be rectified scientifically, from an untenable hypothesis which will fade out, or from a mistaken interpretation of the truths contained in the official teachings of the Church. Within their own sphere therefore, the experts have complete liberty for their research work.

The famous historical interventions of the Church *à propos* of publications touching on scientific facts, astronomical, geological, palaeontological and so on have always been caused by the publicity, premature for the general public, given to hypotheses not yet proven. The Church does not hinder experts and specialists from pursuing their investigations, even when these seem to weaken some of its traditional teachings. It asks them however to abstain from rashly throwing out, into minds not prepared for them, opinions which are still purely hypothetical, and which could cause unjustifiable anxiety. This was the case, during the course of history, with the new theories put out on the subject of the earth's rotation, of creation over periods incomparably longer than the six days of Genesis, of evolutionary theory and of the use in the Pentateuch of documents much earlier in date than that of the final version.

Directly the Church knew that these facts had been established as scientifically certain, it accepted the necessity of adopting not its dogmatic or moral teaching, which is outside the sphere of science, but the traditional interpretation of this or that Scriptural formula.

A theologian would agree with Professor William Mackenzie's formula in his lecture on the limits of parapsychology, *La Métapsychique*, 1904-46, Vol. 1, p. 4 ("Parapsychology," 1904-46): "Beyond phenomenal and sensible nature there is only the illimitable field of action of metaphysical and philosophical thought in general, or of religious feeling, which develop freely in the transphenomenal world intelligible to those of understanding. Our science, on the contrary, is like all the others an infinitely more modest affair. Its aims are to observe without prejudice and, before anything else, to verify the reality of phenomena: then to experiment as much as possible, with the object of discovering and establishing what conditions are necessary and sufficient to produce such phenomena; to work out the consequences, the correspondences and eventually the constant factors inherent in these data; finally, to classify the phenomena themselves, seeking wherever possible to fit newly observed facts into the categories of facts already known." Such purely scientific objectives could not disquiet Catholic orthodoxy.

But the Church could not refrain from reacting against the incursions of parapsychologists who, quitting the scientific terrain, may penetrate directly or indirectly into the realm of religion or morals, or publicize philosophical hypotheses whose implications are fundamentally opposed to revealed doctrine.

Thus the Church could not admit that all possibility of intervention by a discarnate being must be excluded. Naturally the scientist as such does not have to take miracles into account; but neither must he exclude them, nor deny that they may happen. He must be ready to recognize the limits of his researches if a day comes when they cannot succeed in explaining a phenomenon, while the religious circumstances lead the believer to envisage the hypothesis of a supernatural intervention.

It has been shown that at Lourdes the *Bureau des Constatations* does not have to affirm, or to grant recognition to miracles; all it does is to give the religious authorities the dossier proving the reality of a cure inexplicable in scientific terms, and so paranormal. It would however be going outside the jurisdiction of medical science to reject the possibility of a miraculous intervention of God.

In the same way, in studying premonitions, clairvoyance, palmistry, astrology and kindred subjects, the Church could not admit explanations which in practice deny the existence of free will. It is the task of parapsychology to test the reality of such phenomena as predictions, or precognitions of the future which are exactly fulfilled. To build philosophical or occultist theories on these facts would be to leave the sphere of science for that of religion.

The Catholic Church could not moreover allow it to be maintained that the dead really intervene as a result of evocations other than prayer, and of proceedings forbidden by God in the Bible and many times afterwards prohibited by the Church herself.

Parapsychologists cannot set forth doctrines concerning the fate of the dead, their reincarnation and so forth without leaving the field of scientific activity and attacking Christian religious doctrine.

Such divagations as these being excluded, the Church is

very anxious to see psychical research developing in a spirit of perfect objectivity, and without prejudices of any kind.

For these studies, if carried on by genuine experts, with all the necessary critical detachment, can help considerably in the research work carried on by theologians specializing in the field of mysticism and in the study of divine or diabolical marvels: by tracing frauds and deceptions and devising methods of detecting them; by bringing to light natural explanations of paranormal phenomena which have mistakenly been attributed to preternatural causes; by helping to delimit the boundaries of the authentically marvellous.

After having detailed the valuable services rendered to the study of miraculous cures by the *Bureau des Constatations Médicales de Lourdes,* and the special Commission of the Sacred Congregation of Rites, one is drawn to wish that similar commissions of experts not confined to any one diocese could be set up to investigate and study all the phenomena of visions, apparitions, stigmatizations which are proliferating today; phenomena for which the diocesan ecclesiastical authorities have not always suitable investigators, since only specialized training and long practical experience can fit men to discover the truth, in view of all the obstacles described in Chapter II. Theoretical science, the utmost good faith and a religious spirit may not avail to detect those fantastic deceptions, conscious or unconscious, which surround faked phenomena.

CHAPTER IV

CONCLUSIONS OR CONTEMPORARY SCIENTIFIC OPINIONS

Is it now possible to speak of scientific conclusions in connection with psychical research? Are there paranormal phenomena whose genuineness has been established with such stringent accuracy that their occurrence can be taken for granted as definitely proven; paranormal phenomena concerning which different groups of parapsychologists and psychical research workers are in full agreement? Are there, on the other hand, varieties of phenomena which are always attributable to fraud, and which have been exposed so frequently that all further instances of them should henceforward be excluded from the sphere of scientific research and relegated to the domain of conjuring tricks?

In order to draw up the balance sheet of contemporary studies in parapsychology, we shall distinguish phenomena which seem to be physico-chemical in nature ("physical phenomena" in the English usage) from psychological phenomena. It may seem a little arbitrary to classify data in these two categories, but to do so contributes towards clarity of exposition, and corresponds with contemporary methods of observing, assessing and grouping cases.

In the first category will be grouped the phenomena of psycho-kinesis (movements caused by the soul without the intermediary of nerves and muscles) or telekinesis (movements carried out at a distance, without contact or transmitting instruments[1]); levitations, the transfer of objects from one position to another, poltergeist hauntings; then materializations or the extrusion of ectoplasm; in addition, all the material and physiological marvels which yogis claim to produce; finally magnetism, or the action of supposedly objective fluids exhaled by the human organism.

Into the second category will come the data regarding extrasensory perception: thought transmission, telepathy, clairvoyance, psychometry; predictions and premonitions; astrology; and the phenomena of psychological automatism, automatic writing, drawing, painting.

PHYSICAL PHENOMENA

Psycho-kinesis or Telekinesis, Levitation, Transference of Objects, Poltergeist Hauntings

If we consider first of all phenomena experimentally induced under laboratory conditions, the balance of results in the physical category will be found poor and meagre.

Occurrences of the sort hitherto believed to be well-authenticated have diminished in direct proportion to the development of new methods and new scientific devices for investigation, designed to eliminate opportunities both of error and of fraud. If we abide only by the most recent conclusions of psychical research in the "paraphysical" domain, we shall be left with an impression of disappointment.

We shall do no more than mention the attitude of the Belgian Committee (cf. p. 36 above) towards physical phenomena. Its members, qualified experts in their various fields, are definite and categorical in their denial of objective reality to physical phenomena said to be effected by the will without direct or instrumental contact exercised by the body upon the

[1] The term psycho-kinesis or PK is used by some authorities for both forms of activity to which distance seems irrelevant. [*Trans.*]

object moved or modified.[1] Julien Tondriau (*Fakirisme physique*, 1952 ("Physical Wizardry") declares (p. 8): "All typtology is trickery, achieved by the use of threads, automatic machinery, physico-chemical reactions, etc". Readers may know that the word typtology indicates single inexplicable noises apparently producing themselves at a distance from any human being.

He adds: "Levitation is no more than sleight of hand . . . in 1931 an official prize of 50,000 francs (of much more value in those days) was offered in Paris to whomsoever could move without touching it a pencil placed upon a glass tray; control conditions were postulated." No one tried the experiment.

After these completely negative conclusions should be cited those of Robert Amadou, more delicately shaded but still disappointing. This former Director of *La Revue métapsychique* had at his disposal not only all the publications of the I.M.I. (International Parapsychological Institute) but also the archives in which are recorded word for word the proceedings of all the *séances* in which Dr Geley and Dr Osty, successive Presidents of this Institute, experimented with such length and care to test the telekinetic powers of world famous physical mediums. In *La Parapsychologie*, 1954, p. 71, he wrote:

"No one can maintain that the paranormal phenomena attributed to physical mediums do not occur. But no one accustomed to using the scientific methods proper to modern psychical research can maintain without qualification that they are genuine. After ruling out certain indubitable frauds, it is possible to argue about the greater or lesser probability of cheating or of illusion in this or that particular case. But one can never be sure that such a probability can in any circumstances be altogether excluded. Experiments carried out with great mediums have never resulted in absolute proof of the existence of paranormal physical phenomena; and only

[1] It should perhaps be noted that in *psi* phenomena of all kinds subconscious attention and attraction seem to be the effective factors rather than the conscious assertion of will power.

absolute proof has any scientific value. Whether physical phenomena of the kind which great mediums were believed to produce occur or not, none has ever been produced or repeated under conditions capable of convincing the expert. We should hesitate to deny the existence of paranormal physical phenomena. Nevertheless, we must put on record the fact that no absolute proof of the occurrence of such phenomena has ever been achieved."

After noting that "former experimental work, imperfect and piecemeal, urges us to reserve judgement", Robert Amadou invites parapsychologists to begin experimenting and making observation again, with more detachment and more stringent precautions. That such a view can be held by one of the best informed personalities of today about psychical research problems, a personality with access to such rich documentary sources, leaves us puzzled and on our guard.

What certain and positive results have been achieved by the innumerable sequences of more or less public experiments and *séances* carried on at the International Parapsychological Institute, or at the French Association for Parapsychological Studies? Where are the present-day successors of the mediums famous half a century ago, Eusapia Palladino, Douglas Home, Florence Cook, Eva C., Stella C., Jean Guzik, the brothers Willy and Rudi Schneider, who were frequently observed by psychical research workers of high standing, and whose psycho-kinetic powers were celebrated in the press throughout the world?

It looks as if the line were extinct, and as if the progress of parapsychological science, and of technical means of detecting fraud had brought about its complete disappearance. Psychical research journals, instead of describing modern experiments, discuss over again the findings of twenty or thirty years ago and more; this is remarkable in view of the improvement in methods of psychical research which has taken place of late years. Otherwise these journals confine themselves to the subject of paranormal phenomena in the psychological field, the extra-sensory perceptions which are absolutely the order of the day.

The President of the French Association for Parapsychological Studies (*Association Française d'Etudes Métapsychiques*), Vicomte Bertrand de Cressac, in his turn draws very limited and cautious conclusions in *La Métapsychique devant la Science* ("Parapsychology and Science"), Paris, Dervy, 1948, p. 135. "Even more than with phenomena of an intellectual order, the parapsychologist who wishes scientifically to study parapsychological phenomena with physical consequences, must have as his motto 'make haste slowly'. In point of fact, despite the enormous volumes of observations and experiments of all kinds undertaken in order to investigate such phenomena, the fastidious scientist can so far glean little from them."

He too expresses regret at having to remark on the insufficiency of previous experiments in psychical research of this kind.

Dr Rhine expressed a similar opinion in March 1946; it is recorded thus by R. Amadou (*op. cit.*, p. 72): "It would be impossible to collect from previous research work a dossier of evidence proving the occurrence of PK (psycho-kinesis). There were not enough controls, not enough trials, not enough observations. New experiments are needed, with better methods of control."

Such are the most recent attitudes of parapsychologists in connection with paranormal physical phenomena, as experimentally induced in laboratories or at the very least in the presence of qualified scientific observers. Should it then be concluded that the phenomena of levitation, the unexplained movement of objects, etc., remain completely unproven, and should be considered impossible unless further evidence becomes available? Not at all.

Beyond such phenomena as can be reproduced in laboratory conditions under specialized control, history both ancient and modern, and current events themselves, provide examples of a very large number of incidents occurring without human forethought or preparation, quite unexpectedly, often taking people completely unawares, and occurring in the presence of numerous and trustworthy witnesses.

It would be unreasonable to dismiss *en bloc* all the facts set out in the lives of saints, or at any rate of holy persons, past and present; levitations during the course of an ecstasy in which the body is sometimes lifted visibly to a considerable height in the sight of a large number of people; the phenomena of bilocation (better known in England as that of phantasms of the living) allowing the body, or the body image, to show itself and even to act at a great spatial distance; the miraculous apports of far off objects, etc. In the same way, in cases of true diabolic possession, often during the course of the exorcism itself, the body has been lifted into the air or been thrown violently about.

In cases of houses haunted by poltergeists, cases which have abounded from the earliest ages to our own, physical phenomena have been described by large numbers of witnesses including official observers, detectives, constables, police superintendents and clergy in responsible positions whose circumstantial reports we possess.

Parapsychologists object that the phenomena of poltergeist haunting have but rarely been studied by competent persons, able to exert those methods of control which are indispensable if mistakes are to be prevented. Robert Amadou draws attention to the fact that Dr Geley, President of the *Institut Métapsychique International*, was only once asked to test the authenticity of such an occurrence. He went to the site of it with Charles Richet; but with no result. During the course of eleven years another of its Presidents, Dr Osty, was not even once called upon to verify such phenomena. It is easily explained. Poltergeist hauntings are of such a character that the victims instinctively appeal not to scientific investigators but to the police or to a priest. For everything combines to make them think they are being pursued by a malign entity —or at least a teasing one—which amuses itself by annoying, worrying or frightening them.

Setting aside the very frequent cases of more or less conscious trickery (we have ourselves discovered and put a stop to many of these) there are some instances which seem to be genuine and cannot be explained except by the intervention of some entity foreign to man.[1] This is the suggestion made by Count Emile Tizane, who has compiled so many police dossiers on poltergeist hauntings. In *Sur la piste de l'homme inconnu* ("On the Track of Unknown Man"), p. 64, he writes: "All these phenomena lead one to admit the action of a power invisible, intelligent, malicious, very skilful, gifted with a ready wit, and responding sometimes, as if to amuse itself, to the desires of those present."

There is one circumstance which recurs in all these spontaneous marvels and which modifies hypotheses as to their nature by referring them to a sphere beyond the grasp of scientific parapsychology. This circumstance, this inevitable context, is the supernatural aspect of antecedent or concomitant phenomena, which implant in the mind a conviction that a factor outside the natural order is at work, an entity which eludes scientific control.

It is the part of parapsychological science to verify exactly what has happened, and to seek for a natural explanation, normal or paranormal, but the supernatural is beyond its range; it can neither prove nor disprove its existence nor organize an experimental repetition of the phenomena to which it gives rise. Let us not enter the province of theology.

Materializations. Ectoplasm

By these terms are meant materializations of the spirits of the dead, or even of the living, appearing in more or less complete darkness, or leaving traces of their presence such as the mould of a hand in paraffin wax. Ectoplasm is a hypothetical substance of an unknown kind visible in a dim light, which exudes and separates itself from the medium, and takes on shapes resembling those of the human face or body.

For a long time these phenomena attracted and retained

[1] It should perhaps be said that in England and the United States such cases are sometimes attributed to the projection of subconscious conflicts in telekinetic form. [*Trans.*]

the attention of spiritualist circles and of those who organized psychical research *séances*. Books and periodicals specializing in revelations of the marvellous have indeed published many mysterious photographs of ectoplasm. But so much trickery has been discovered in this connection (the use of phosphorescent products, impregnated gauze, buttermuslin, chemical vapour and so on) that the real existence of ectoplasm seems less and less probable. This is a field where conjuring reigns supreme.

Robert Tocquet in *Tout l'occultisme devoilé* ("Occultism Unveiled"), 1952, says: "Ectoplasmic phenomena are certainly the most doubtful constituents of the data of parapsychology. They are easy to imitate, frequently faked, hard to fit into the framework of our psycho-physical knowledge, absurd, almost inconceivable. It is obviously difficult for all these reasons to suppose that they exist at all as authentically paranormal occurrences." He thinks, though, basing his judgement on accounts dating from the beginning of this century, that occasional instances may be genuine. These accounts however go back at least fifty years, to a time before contemporary methods of investigation were developed. How would ectoplasm look to an electronic eye?

Robert Amadou, who has been able to study the reports of experiments made by his predecessors at the *Institut Métapsychique International*, has not devoted a single paragraph to this subject in his work on parapsychology. Photographs of ectoplasm should be put into the same category as spirit photography, which we have never been able to take seriously.[1] Photographic experts discovered the origin of these quite early on. Beginners in photography are particularly favoured by them; defective focusing, movements of the camera, the superimposition of two images upon one negative explain many strange but quite natural pictures.

[1] Perhaps it should be said that accurate photographs of this kind sometimes show, if sufficiently enlarged, the weave of the buttermuslin employed, a weave perhaps more familiar to the housewife than to the professional research worker. [*Trans.*]

Yoga

There is nothing paranormal about the phenomena so ostentatiously paraded by those in Europe who have brought almost into ridicule the reputation and the mission of true yogis. It is well known that these Hindu ascetics pursue not publicity but personal holiness, by methods of prayer and physical mortification intended so to master and train the body that the spirit may be uplifted to the contemplation of divine truth.

The origin of these ascetic modes of purification and of sharpening the faculty for mystical experience lies very far back in ancient religions. Under different but kindred forms these procedures adopted by Gnosticism are to be found in India as in Egypt or Greece, among the priestly caste of Brahmins as among wandering fakirs. It is unnecessary to discuss the religious aspect of these practices; enough to note here that they lead to the development of insensitiveness to the pain caused by wounds or burns, and of conscious control of the respiratory, digestive and circulatory systems. These ascetics reduce to a surprising minimum the normal needs of the human organism.

On the other hand they acquire a strength of will, and a power of perception and of suggestion which enable them to exert a quite exceptional influence on those around them. Seen thus, they have been the object of fascinating parapsychological investigations of those paranormal powers which man can acquire and develop by purely natural methods. The Congress of Royaumont (May 1956) studied this problem at some length. It does not come within the scope of this book.

This aspect of true yoga has nothing in common with those self-styled yogis, Hindu or otherwise, who have organized so many publicity turns to exhibit their positively astounding powers of invulnerability, incombustibility, catalepsy, prolonged fasting, the suspension of breathing, etc. Lying on beds of nails, climbing ladders whose rungs are swords, walking on broken glass and the plunging of needles or even daggers into the body; all these have nothing to do with parapsychology.[1]

Conjuring is the explanation of all these achievements, and the conjurer can repeat them in public at will.

If any reader needs up-to-date knowledge of how these classical tricks are performed, he should read chapter twelve of Robert Tocquet's *Tout l'occultisme devoilé* (1954); it deals fully with this subject. The Belgian Committee already cited published in 1952 two pamphlets by Julien Tondriac, Director of History, Philosophy and Letters, on *Prétendus Mystères du Fakirisme* ("So-called Mysteries of Yoga") which shows how innumerable tricks of this sort are worked.

But pseudo-yogis will always be popular with people who prefer thrills to facts, illusions to commonplace reality. This book is not written for them.

Magnetism, Current and Waves

All those paranormal physico-chemical phenomena whose genuineness is maintained by believers in the physical powers of mediums can be explained, we are told, by the existence of a human current capable of causing vibrations, auras, waves, magnetic disturbances, etc. Many healers and radiesthetists explain their work in the terms of this famous current.

It is obvious that the latest opinions of parapsychological experts as to this current will be of especial interest.

It should be noted at once that the word can carry two quite different meanings.

The "current" could be a reality of a philosophical kind, a metaphysical concept transcending the sphere of experimental science, which could therefore neither establish nor analyse it. This hypothetical "current" appears in various philosophical, occultist or religious systems as something superior to matter; either purely spiritual or of an order

[1] This is doubtful. If parapsychology is based on ordinary psychology there is no reason to exclude instances of psychosomatic or hysterical anaesthesia from its subject matter. Thus fire walking is a well-attested phenomenon, and pricking suspected witches with a pin was an old test; if they did not feel it, they were judged guilty. [*Trans.*]

intermediary between spirit and matter. It would be a kind of world-soul permeating and directing all things. This idea is found in Eastern religions and in Polynesia, where the force is known as *Mana*, and also among the ancient Greeks, the theosophists, the disciples of Mesmer and the followers of Allan Kardec. Certain spiritualist healers claim that they use this vital "current" to bring about cures. This religious or philosophical concept of the "current" does not belong to the sphere of parapsychological science. We need not linger over it.

But there is another definition of this "current" which brings it fully within the orbit of psychical research. In this case the term denotes a physical aura emanating from the living body, and manifesting itself in different sorts of psycho-kinetic activity (in acting on organs and living tissues so as to stimulate healing), and in playing a decisive part in extra-sensory perception, especially where radiesthesia is concerned. This "current", again, is said to stimulate the germination of seeds, and speed up their growth, to destroy germs, and to ensure the preservation of foodstuffs that are in the normal way highly perishable (meat, fish, etc.).

The question of its existence has already been raised by Charles Richet (p. 123): "It is possible that this radiation exists, since everything is possible; but up till now no one has been able to demonstrate it. The existence of a vital current, a magnetic emanation has never been conclusively shown."

What does contemporary psychical research say about the subject? In 1953 *La Revue métapsychique* devoted an entire issue to this problem: *Le Fluide* (No. 21), 90 pages. The various authors are extremely cautious in view of the uncertain results achieved by serious experiments in connection with this question.

Thus René Dufour (p. 72): "Doubtful reality, equivocal concept, ill-chosen word, this is the judgement we are led to pass on the idea of the current as such; and yet all this is associated in fact with a multiplicity of authentic phenomena."

Robert Amadou quotes a reply made by Dr Pascal (p. 31):

"In the present state of science, there is nothing to prove the existence of the magnetic fluid."

René Hardy recounts a series of strictly scientific experiments on the so-called "current" of radiesthetists and healers, in which the results quite simply correspond with those of the calculus of probability. (p. 79) "Investigations of the action of the 'current' on the different kinds of apparatus described, and on others, including extremely sensitive amplifiers which we set up for the purpose have still not enabled us to furnish evidence of any special emanation proceeding from healers which has anything to do with the cures they effect, even though these may be quite real."

In his book *La Parapsychologie* Robert Amadou comes to negative conclusions. In connection with photographs of human emanations (p. 67) he makes a critical analysis of the famous experiments of Reichenbach and De Rochas presented to the Academy of Sciences in 1897, and of that of Dr Baraduc, who obtained a photograph of the "radiation of the Blessed Sacrament at the moment of a miraculous cure". Guy de Fontenay showed in a startling fashion that it was no more than a question of the chemical effects of heat, or of the secretion of sweat; by heating the hand of a corpse to a certain temperature he obtained photographs of radiations more strongly marked than those from a living hand.

In the same way MM. de Saint Albin and Warcollier, and Dr Menager, after a very extensive series of experiments came to the conclusion that "the emanations photographed are no more than pseudo-emanations brought about by heat, acting as such and as a source of movement".

As for "auras", those halos surrounding the heads of mediums and other human beings, Robert Amadou concludes (p. 68): "The objective existence of auras has never been proved."

Branly, and then Warcollier, President of the I.M.I., were able to ascertain that various instruments and pieces of apparatus which seem to register vibrations emanating from the human organism did no more than record the variation of body heat and the movements that it brought about. Slight tremors of the body set the needle moving, giving a false impression of magnetic activity. Other apparatus, including Dr Albert Leprince's radiobarometer noted nothing more than the normal electrical variations of the organism.

Professor Jordan, who teaches theoretical physics at the University of Hamburg, declared at the conversations of Saint-Paul-de-Vence, in 1954: "Neither modern nor traditional physics gives the slightest support to those champions of a strange 'fluid' who believe in waves and radiations of a kind so far unknown. On the contrary, both challenge the validity of such hypotheses, which stand in direct opposition to what is known of physical reality."

The existence and nature of this fluid therefore remain problematical. To note René Hardy's wise observations, "It is quite certain that no one has yet tabulated all the modes of manifesting energy inherent in the human being, and someone will probably find a more direct method—and simple apparatus—for testing the individual's potential vitality than that of comparing various measurements. It is the function of the laboratory to show whether some particular form of energy emanating from the hands, more especially from the finger tips, can be assessed and measured; if so, this form of energy will be included in the concepts of classical physiological physics." Let us not take for paranormal what is no more than a little known manifestation of perfectly natural energy varying in intensity from one individual to another.

What is to be thought of healers who, appealing to their hypothetical "current", produce unmistakable natural cures?

The appeal to a current or fluid is only one of many different procedures adopted by healers in order to effect improvements or cures. The procedure does not matter much; what counts is the power of suggestion exerted by these magnetizers. They act on the patient's subconscious mind and achieve what Pierre Janet called "psychological medication".

I have described it elsewhere.[1] The fluid is no more efficacious than many other prescriptions, some absurd or even hurtful in themselves, used by the healers who flourish today, or by the doctors of former times or backward countries. The fact of having "felt" the heat which seems to be released from the healer's hands (a heat whose nature has not so far been elucidated) serves as a powerful vehicle through which benevolent suggestion can be transmitted to the patient's psyche.

Medical psychologists are well aware of the enormous part played by the psyche in the course of sickness and of recovery, and psycho-somatic medicine is developing fast. The Order of Doctors[2] is attempting to protect official medicine with its purely material cures. The healer is very often, consciously or otherwise, using psychological medicine.

PSYCHOLOGICAL PHENOMENA

Here we approach a terrain where psychical research has much more of a harvest than in the field of physical phenomena where the yield is infinitesimal. Parapsychologists increasingly confine their attention to this. In fact it seems likely that they will increasingly abandon the study of so-called paranormal physical phenomena for the attempt to establish and to investigate the psychological data more thoroughly.

Many of them no longer have any doubt that such phenomena really occur. It will therefore be plain that in this connection we can record much less disappointing conclusions.

[1] Réginald-Omez, O.P., *Que penser des guérisseurs* (Présences, 1955), No. 50.

[2] The Order of Doctors was established in France in 1940, during the German Occupation; but it had often been discussed before the war, from 1845 onwards in fact. This Order, suppressed at the Liberation, was refounded in September 1945. It is a useful safeguard against the grave dangers of amateur treatment, but it would be a pity if it became on occasion the protector of doctors at the expense of their patients, or if it prevented the use of the wonderful resources of suggestion in treatment above all when these resources are used or supervised by qualified medical men.

Note at the outset the following reassuring declaration by Robert Amadou: "The existence of supposedly paranormal physical phenomena has not been scientifically established. On the other hand, thought transference, telepathy, clairvoyance, or to speak more accurately, the behaviour and experiences to which these words refer, have been scientifically proved, though their mode of operation has not yet been made clear."

Extra-sensory Perception

Parapsychologists indicate by the expression *psi*, the function at work in all paranormal phenomena, including psycho-kinesis. In Anglo-American usage extra-sensory perception, or ESP denotes (as it implies) the phenomena of paranormal knowledge, thought transmission, telepathy, clairvoyance, psychometry, radiesthesia and so on.

Of late years it is ESP which has attracted the most attention in parapsychological studies. Books and periodicals treat it as of overriding importance. The Congress of Utrecht in 1953 and the conversations of Saint-Paul-de-Vence in 1954 devoted almost all their reports and discussions to ESP phenomena.

This time the conclusions are no longer either negative or reduced to a few slender hypotheses. Psychical research has at least unearthed one precious vein of ore. We may note some of the most firmly established findings.

First of all, we can consider the phenomena of telepathy, or the transmission of thought.

There have always been instances of this which forced themselves upon the mind: spontaneous instances, easy to verify, of the innumerable telepathic messages emitted by dying persons. Scientists, ancient and modern, have turned away from such reports as anecdotes which it is impossible either to examine or to explain. Religious persons, or spiritualists, or occultists have envisaged them as interventions by discarnate beings, souls already separated from the body, which had nothing to do with science.

But to these appeals or warnings from the dying must be added many analogous cases in which the person sending the message is not dead; the unexpected transmission of pain, anxiety, sudden joy or hope. This has moreover happened in circumstances in which the phenomenon can be verified; the person perceiving it has in fact instantly spoken of his vision to others who have then been able to establish its more or less complete correspondence with the real event that has taken place at the same time, often at a considerable distance.

Such matters are of course somewhat frustrating to the laboratory parapsychologist who can neither record nor analyse them. Nevertheless, he cannot deny their existence. J. B. Rhine remarks (*op. cit.*, p. 30): "Perhaps I have not yet said often enough that it would be scientifically unthinkable to consider any of these reports of spontaneous occurrences as acceptable proof of anything . . . (but) when enough people say the same kind of thing, no matter how strange and incredible it may be, it is wise to look into the facts, letting the interpretation wait. . . . How can progress be made if all the puzzling things that occur in nature are ignored, and if scientists refuse to study what they cannot at once explain, and what some people call impossible." This makes sense.

For my own part, I have often had occasion to verify, after the closest scrutiny, the reality of telepathic messages which were wholly inexplicable in terms either of coincidence or of fraud.

Psychical research workers have tried to establish the reality of such phenomena by planned experiments in thought transference which we shall now consider.

We have described the two methods, quantitative and qualitative, which are used in such research. The results obtained by the quantitative method have been mathematically conclusive. Professor Rhine's experiments, which ran to 3,600,634 trials, eliminating all conceivable counter hypotheses, established the fact that extra-sensory perception really exists. The Pratt-Woodruff experiments in 1939, with 60,000 trials also produced proofs conclusive by statistical standards. The Vicomte de Cressac, president of the *Association Française des Etudes Métapsychiques* (The French Association for Parapsychological Studies) organized an experimental demonstration of telepathy and, out of 1000 trials with two series of forty cards with different pictures, achieved 258 perfect successes, where the calculus of probability would have predicted no more than 249. It would be possible to quote numerous similar pieces of research work which have produced approximately similar results.

They fully justify the remarks of Dr Schaefer, Professor of Physiology and Director of the Physiology Laboratory at the University of Heidelberg, who declared at the Utrecht Congress: "Rhine's experiments have proved the existence of parapsychological phenomena in so far as telepathy and clairvoyance are concerned."

This was to proclaim the reality of thought transference phenomena, whatever the distance might be, and of clairvoyance in its many forms; psychometry, mediumism, radiesthesia. Directly the possibility of thought transference is admitted, a first element of hypothetical explanation for these phenomena has been found.

Once the existence of extra-sensory perception was proved, the parapsychologists strove to find an explanation. What is the nature of this perception? What are its vectors or vehicles, what organs transmit and receive it?[1]

Here there are still no conclusions, nothing but hypotheses based rather on philosophy or occultism, than on experimental work. Contemporary parapsychologists recognize that, as Dr Thouless said in 1952, we are still occupied in "formulating systems of hypotheses leading to certain suppositions which it will be possible to submit to the criterion of experiment".

[1] Its name conveys of course, to the English reader, that it is not connected with sense organs at all. But cf. *Nature* for July 1951, and subsequent issues for an essay and correspondence on the relations between mind and brain. [*Trans.*]

And after reading Soal and Bateman, *Modern Experiments in Telepathy*, Sir Julian Huxley too declared: "All these occurrences are still totally inexplicable; but during the last twenty years it has been established that they do in fact happen." This is not much. But such is the view of all serious contemporary parapsychologists. Robert Amadou pleads in favour of this modest science: "Parapsychology is the youngest of all human sciences, and the objects of its study are not the easiest to seize or elucidate."

In examining these facts we have at last been able to note some typical details, some characteristic circumstances which could help us to discover something of their nature.

Charles Richet observed that the phenomena of extra-sensory perception did not seem to be confined only to certain types of person: "We know that some people are more gifted than others, but also that no one is without some degree of cryptaesthesia, however faint it may be."

Contemporary parapsychologists admit that the *psi*-function is probably universal. It is easy to see, indeed, that the phenomena of telepathy, second sight, veridical presentiments and so on occur among people of very different gifts and temperaments. There are certainly some people who have such experiences more often than others. But some who have never previously shown any sensitiveness to them are sometimes favoured, on an exceptional occasion, with telepathic communications of extraordinary clarity and accuracy. Those gifted with second sight or with a talent for thought reading do not always show an aptitude for other forms of extra-sensory perception, or other behaviour patterns which might make it possible to recognize any special sensory or mental predisposition to such activities.

Moreover, telepathic perceptions can be observed in a high degree of development among animals, dogs for instance; who show it not only in connection with man, but with their fellows whose sufferings, anxieties or appeals for help they perceive from great distances.

We can therefore assert that these phenomena do not seem

to be exclusively reserved to certain human beings, highly gifted, supersensitive or subjected to the influence of alien beings. Paranormal cognition, as found in all human individuals and in at least a very large number of animals, is a natural thing, though the various perceptions comprised in it seem to be facilitated by certain special tendencies like those of mediums and clairvoyants.

Among certain people there is to be found a more accentuated and a more efficient *psi*-function; the gift of second sight. R. Warcollier, now President of the *Institut Métapsychique International*, believes that "everyone of good faith who has experimented with clairvoyant subjects is obliged to acknowledge that these subjects very easily put themselves psychically into touch with people at greater or lesser distances, above all, if they are known to the experimenter" (*La Métapsychique* 1940-46).

It is well known, on the other hand, what an enormous proportion of these subjects is tainted, to a greater or less degree, with hysteria or neuroses producing a morbid hypersensitivity.

Careful observation of the activities of mediums and clairvoyants shows at once that the greatest number of extrasensory phenomena take place when the percipient is in a special state of psychological dissociation which sets the subconscious free from the control of the conscious self. This state is characterized by the relaxation of attention, a sort of withdrawal from one's surroundings, an abandonment of conscious control, all bringing about what is called the condition of trance.

This will be found, in various degrees of intensity, in all manifestations of mediumism; in the preliminary approach to table-turning as well as in that to the ouija board, automatic writing, radiesthesia, psychometry and so on. The operator must always put himself into a state of relaxation, of recollection, which consists in receptiveness rather than activity, of passiveness rather than tension. It is important to extinguish, or at any rate to reduce as far as possible, all psychological consciousness, in order to allow the subconscious to level up, to take over control uninhibited by any reflex censorship or exercise of will power, and to show itself without any interference from the "I", which has been crowded out. It is then that the "Other Self" comes into its own, with its unfathomable richness of perception and all its spontaneous associations of imagery.

The more a person is carried away, the more quickly will he enter into this trance state, in the same way as people accustomed to putting themselves to sleep by autosuggestion very soon come to be able to enter a state of slumber rapidly and at will.

Entry into trance can be the result of a voluntary effort to relax all tension; as when, unable to remember a word, a name, a date, one says, "Don't think any more, don't bother about it, it will come back of its own accord", in order to let the subconscious continue its investigations alone, undisturbed by the voluntary effort of memory. This trance concentration is remarkable in that it is not a tense struggle towards a given object, already seen, on which the eye of the imagination is focused; it is above all an effort to abstract oneself from all sensations, all intellectual constructions, all images, in order to become entirely passive and receptive to the subconscious.

Trance requires that we should not be tense in any way, that we should abstain completely from conscious thought or voluntary imaginings. Otherwise we paralyse the activity of the subconscious, and prevent paranormal cognition bursting through all the more or less conscious sensations and images which quiver within us.

A large number of the setbacks which occur in the organized and scientifically checked experiments in clairvoyance, telepathy, radiesthesia are no doubt to be explained thus. The very fact of being watched by critical or even sceptical observers, with the anxiety that this provokes, could prevent the achievement of that complete receptivity, that free play of the subconscious, just as fear can paralyse the memory. The slightest ripples on the surface of a lake prevent its reflecting faithfully the trees which mirror themselves there.

There are on the other hand circumstances which facilitate this sort of duplication of personality and somnolence of the censorship of the conscious mind; for instance prolonged concentration on the "screen" provided by a crystal, on the object used for psychometry, on planchette, on the diviner's pendulum and so forth. Little by little this fixed gaze brings about a sort of weariness, leading to the relaxation of attention, and so leaving the field free for the activity of the subconscious. The object which serves as screen is probably unimportant except in so far as it facilitates the trance condition which allows of contact with the conscious or unconscious thoughts of another person, or even with his memory alone.

The rapping table can play the part of a "screen". An illustration of this is to be found in *Les Tables tournantes de Jersey* ("The Turning Tables of Jersey") by G. Simon. Victor Hugo was present at these spiritualistic experiments from which the following features are quoted:

(P. 288) "An Englishman touching the table, it was English verses which came through";

(P. 286) "Mr Kesler thought of two words and the table dictated them" ;

(P. 283) "Mr Kesler did not touch the table, and thought the word 'dagger', which was given by the table";

(P. 267) "The table quoted an unpublished poem by Victor Hugo, only known to him. Then the poet secretly composed the following lines, writing them down as he did so.

> They tore the saints who on the hurdle died
> Their hideous nails rent wider in His side
> The wound of Christ.

At the same moment the table dictated these lines:

> Their paws tore martyrs who on hurdles died
> And Christ received their nails within His side
> O gibbet, with thy nails."

Here is a very good case of composition by thought transference.

I have several times made identical observations in experiments with the talking glass, the latter dictating words thought intensely by someone who was not touching the glass.[1]

The pendulum in radiesthesia plays at first the part of the "screen" facilitating the entry into trance which conditions extra-sensory perception. The radiesthetist fixes his attention on it, watching for it to begin moving. At the same time as he concentrates his gaze on to this object, disregarding all other sensations, he is making himself more receptive towards the knowledge he seeks. Hence his subconscious can more easily seize hold of the "communication" that is sought. This is then exteriorized by the movements of the pendulum, whose oscillation or rotation demonstrates the impression of illusion of perception felt by the subject: this is the second function of the pendulum.

After having rejected the physico-chemical explanation of radiesthesia (that is, the action exerted on the pendulum by waves or radiations whose existence is now denied by men of science) psychical research workers and a large number of radiesthetists of the new school like Henry de France believe that there are only more or less unconscious perceptions, which the pendulum, as a conventional signalling apparatus, transmits to the conscious mind.

Charles Richet put forward this hypothesis (*op. cit.*, p. 296): "Unconscious muscular movements then, reveal through the divining rod as through the turning table, the vibrations set up in our unconscious intelligence by the emanations from objects."

Is there extra-sensory perception of physical realities? This question is so far unanswered. Diviners assure us that they are able to detect water, metals and the most diverse material objects. Parapsychologists are not so sure. Those of them who admit that certain radiesthetic perceptions are at least

[1] Réginald-Omez, O.P., *Peut-on communiquer avec les morts?* ("Can we Communicate with the Dead?"), pp. 159-164.

probable think that they are more likely to be communications of thought rather than perceptions of material objects.

Similarly with telepathy; it looks, up to now, as if there were no direct vision of distant events as such, but rather communication with the thoughts, feelings, imagery of the person who is undergoing or perceiving those events on the spot.

This was the opinion of Dr Osty. It is still that of Robert Amadou. And this would explain how into clairvoyance and mediumism there sometimes slip errors and distortions proceeding from all that could be grafted on to objective reality by the imagination or the subconscious of those with whom the clairvoyant is in touch. It has even been suggested on occasion that perhaps those who foretell the future perceive chiefly the thoughts, anticipations, desires or fears of their clients, who in consulting them enlighten them. This problem offers a vast unexplored field of investigation to psychical research.

Are these perceptions registered by sense-organs whose existence has not so far been discovered by science, or directly by certain cerebral centres?

We do not at present seem to possess enough data on which to construct an adequate hypothesis. Professor Hans Schaeffer, in his account of *La Théorie scientifique de la Recherche en Parapsychologie* ("The Scientific Theory of Parapsychological Research"), at the Congress of Utrecht in 1953 declared (p. 25) that: "It is obviously impossible to decide at present anything about the possible existence of sensory organs still unknown or about unknown combinations of different sorts."

What is the vehicle of thought transference? No satisfactory conclusion about this subject has yet been reached.

Professor Bykov's hypothesis that a "meta-etheric" energy is emitted by the organism and received by interceptory anatomical devices is still purely speculative. Dr Albert Leprince has not yet been able to furnish any experimental demonstration of his theory of rays emanating from a sensitive spot on the skin of the emitter and being received at the symmetrically opposite spot on the body of the percipient sitting face to face with him.

Here, too, parapsychology has much to discover and explain.

Precognition of the future is one of the most disturbing, and certainly the most mysterious of all forms of paranormal cognition; scholars and philosophers seek in vain for its source in the natural order of things.

Psychical research workers will lay especial stress on the possibility of divining the future through present, already existing causes which prepare and bring it into being, causes which telepathy, working through the subconscious mind of the seer, leads him to recognize intuitively and much more accurately than would be possible by the use of deductive reasoning. It is therefore conceivable that in the trance state men can become aware of premonitory signs, early indications, of certain events more easily than in the ordinary state of reflective attention. St Thomas Aquinas long ago pointed out that by studying dreams doctors can sometimes diagnose diseases whose first faint symptoms could not be seen by examining the patient in his waking hours. But parapsychology acknowledges that it is completely helpless to explain precognition of a future which is not implicit in causes operating in the present; whether because these causes are polyvalent, or because it can only result from unpredictable causes due to chance alone, or because it depends on the decision of various free wills, which cannot be foreseen.

Modern philosophers tend to associate the problem with that of our conception of time. Professor Wentzl, at Saint-Paul-de-Vence in 1954 upheld the thesis that there are two time-dimensions, and Dr Martini, that of multiple space-times, with incessantly increasing dimensions.[1]

But is not this attempt to reduce the future in some obscure way to the present simply a slurring over of the problem of foreknowledge?

Those present at the conversations of Saint-Paul-de-Vence

[1] An idea familiar to English readers through the work of J. W. Dunne.

recognized that precognition of the future remains a mystery, unsolved—and in all probability insoluble—by both philosophy and science.

Must it not be faced that only the hypothesis that entities foreign to man are at work can make sense of the numerous authentic instances of precognition and knowledge of the future?[1] Does not this paranormal phenomenon transcend parapsychology, and indeed all the natural sciences? Are we not obliged to have recourse to the preternatural here? At the present time parapsychology can give no plausible natural explanation for it.

Theology maintains that the foretelling of a future which depends upon choice or chance is reserved to the Godhead, and for those to whom God has revealed it. Is it not overbold for science to try to break through its frontiers? It is well known how firmly the Catholic Church, reiterating the definite prohibitions made in the Old Testament, forbids all attempt to discover the future except by the scientific analysis of its natural causes. All fortune telling is forbidden as a recourse, in spite of God, to beings he condemns, and therefore as a rebellion against him.

ASTROLOGY

Is it legitimate to class astrological prophecies among the paranormal phenomena connected with psychical research, as if horoscopes were not rational constructions from data provided by the objective study of the state of the heavens at such and such a given moment? Astrologers indeed set their predictions before us as if they were dictated by the results of astronomical calculations which permit them exactly to map out the position of the planets in relation to the Zodiac,

[1] Not unless one is prepared to admit that these entities intervene on behalf of animals as well as human beings, and moreover exert themselves through thousands of card experiments to help the percipient guess one card ahead of that being proposed for their attention. The necessity of rethinking our ideas about the nature of time seems a more probable explanation. [*Trans.*]

and to deduce from this information the influences which will be exerted on human beings, "inclining, without forcing them".

We can leave the astronomers and the astrologers to discuss together the accuracy of their calculations and the exactness of their description of the state of the sky during the quarter of an hour in which a birth takes place. This has nothing to do with parapsychology. But has not the latter a right to take a hand when the astrologers begin to define (on what basis?) all the psychical or moral influences of the various planets; and when they no longer devote themselves to plotting out the pattern of the stars in the sky, and its meteorological consequences, with their immediate physical repercussions on the terrestrial globe, but work out the biological, psychological, moral, economic and social horoscopes of individuals or nations?

Is there such a very great difference between the "screen" constituted by the lines of the hand, the crystal or the pack of cards on the one hand, and by the birthday sky on the other? Palmists sometimes use a terminology oddly like that of astrologers, which leads us to believe that there may be close affinities between these two arts of divination. Where are the statistics pointing to the infinitely shaded series of tendencies and of accidents plotted out in horoscopes?

Astrology is therefore to be included in the realm of parapsychology under a heading analogous to that of the other precognitions just discussed. It is plausible to cite it, but no more.

PSYCHOLOGICAL AUTOMATISM

This often looks like a sort of paranormal cognition; when it is seen in experiments in automatic writing, drawing or painting, with the ouija board, the talking glass, the use of a pendulum, suspended above the alphabet, and so on. . . . It would therefore seem that this ought to interest the parapsychologist in that it shows him a mode of extra-sensory perception which automatism does no more than translate and express.

Charles Richet asked himself this question some time ago; his reply was a neutral one. At the present time, when all too many people have allowed themselves to be impressed by the diverse forms of automatic so-called "messages", it is perhaps not idle to quote several observations by this founder of French parapsychology. They date from thirty years ago, but our most recent investigations fully corroborate them.

Speaking of two volumes of messages attributed to Thermotis, daughter of an Egyptian Pharaoh, and published under the title *Le Pharaon Menephtah* ("The Pharaoh Menephtah") he said (p. 94): "One would have to suffer from a sickly and almost criminal credulity to accept these at their face value." And, alluding to other series of messages supposed to come from the dead, he added (p. 95): "The character of this literature of the unconscious is so clear-cut that it is easily recognized. It shows, above all, a tendency to large phrases, mystical and vague, about the destiny of the soul, the imperishable forces of the human soul. These wanderings of the subconscious are always very strongly religious, as if it were a question of tracing the outlines of a new religion, with its own rites and doctrines . . . automatic writings detest precision. They avoid all exact definition, and wallow in platitudes. One might call them the work of poets who do not know what poetry is, of philosophers who know no philosophy, of priests who know nothing of religion" (p. 97). "These are typical somnambulist phenomena. It seems difficult to trace any parapsychological influence in them."

Then, writing of automatic paintings and drawings, Charles Richet said—even then—"One would need a culpable dose of credulity to see anything in them but aesthetic projections of the unconscious."

There is nothing paranormal in all this, any more than there is in our most extravagant dreams or in the delirium of fever. All these things are the material of classical psychology, under the chapter-heading of the subconscious.

CHAPTER V

IS PARAPSYCHOLOGY A SCIENCE OF THE FUTURE?

We have established that parapsychology has not been useful only in clearing up a certain number of illusions, and in reducing the domain of the paranormal. It has verified the existence of a mode of perception whose organs and methods of operation are still unknown to science; and it has defined the position of many problems in its own field, whose solutions may be discovered in the future, though only by genuine experts.

Psychical research, or parapsychology, has therefore a future: up till now it has been satisfied with delimiting its objects, and taking the exact bearings by which its exploratory work must be guided if it is to avoid false problems and to be really fruitful.

Is this as much as to say that it should be *the* science of the future, and that one may look forward to seeing it bring about a revolution in the data of classical psychology, as parapsychologists dreamed at the beginning of the century? Does that mysterious "sixth sense" (the supposed receptive organ for thought-transmission in the phenomena of clairvoyance, mediumism, telepathy, radiesthesia, etc.) permit us to envisage and to hope for an enlargement of the human spirit, a development of its psychological capacities? Ought we to consider it a new power, enriching our natures? Can we, in developing our extra-sensory perceptions, further a progressive evolution of the forces of the human soul?

This is not the opinion of contemporary parapsychologists, primarily because this "sixth sense" seems to resemble a relic of some primitive function dulled by the progress of the other senses whose range has been increased by the brain, in devising such secondary means of communication as reading, writing and the use of mathematical formulae, and of late the telephone, broadcasting and television.

Man's extra-sensory perceptions are astonishingly like those of animals, so far as it is possible to judge of these in action. It looks, however, as if those of animals were more highly developed and more accurate. The kind of cognition which appears among urban men to be paranormal and exceptional, seems to be normal to them, although for the most part science has so far been unable to discover the organs by which it operates.

An awareness of water, sometimes at enormous distances, is common among a number of species, above all in countries where water is scarce. Certain animals cover miles of ground, guided by their instinct,[1] to get at a spring beneath an apparently dried up water course, or a trickle down a mountain side.

The homing pigeon, released in a place where it has never been before, and of which it is therefore completely ignorant, discovers the direction in which its home loft lies hundreds of miles away and flies straight as an arrow towards it, at a dizzy speed. It is known that it does not orientate itself by the sun (for it will do it at night) or by radar (for there are no echoes by which to steer at such a height). Bees return to their hive, and wasps to their nest, sometimes deeply buried beneath a disused molehill; and all this in spite of rain or contrary winds, and even in the dark.

The swallow steers itself across thousands of miles of space

[1] Probably a hypersensitive sense of smell; compare human beings who can "smell snow coming". This is surely also the explanation of the work of police dogs cited on the next page; as of the male insect's ability to trace the female, and the ichneumon fly's recognition that a larva already contains an egg. [*Trans.*]

to find its nest, or even the site of a nest destroyed during the course of the winter.

Certain male insects perceive the presence of a female that has emerged from the chrysalis at a great distance from them.

The police dog discovers the tracks, sometimes very long and complicated ones, left by one specific individual, ignoring the traces of numerous others, and all this after several hours have gone by.

The bat perceives and avoids the obstacle, sometimes as thin as a telephone wire, placed on its aerial route while it chases mosquitoes or nightflying moths through the dim evening air; it is believed to be equipped with a natural radar apparatus.

The ichneumon fly is aware in some way that an egg has already been laid in a larva by one of its fellows, and does not lay another one there. It behaves moreover as if it were conscious of the exact position of the relevant motor-nervous centre in its victim and pierces it to reduce to immobility that larva which must continue to live for some time, so that the parasitic young ichneumon may develop within it.

The transmission of orders among creatures living in a group, and working communally on construction, defence and food-gathering, argues that a quite extraordinary degree of telepathy must exist among them (witness Eugène Marais's study of the white ant); as does again, the choice of the underground site of a wasps' nest, and the perfect construction of its comb, with its thousands of symmetrical cells. Among bees, the communication of thought seems often to be accompanied or stimulated by a sort of mimed language. Both English and French readers have probably heard of the remarkable work of Karl von Frisch, of Munich University, who, after forty years of study, discovered a bee-language. By a variety of dances, some tracing semi-circles, and some frisking over a fixed spot, the worker bees indicate the direction and distance of the booty of which they have brought a sample home. These dances show an immediate consciousness of the polarization of light, with which humans have only become acquainted through scientific experiment and deduction.

What is to be thought of instinctive precognition, such as that which seems to warn animals who have never experienced an earthquake, and live in a zone where they are rare, that one is on the way? Such animals have been observed to become anxious, to make sounds of alarm, and to seek shelter long before the earthquake in fact begins.

Migrating birds sometimes become aware of an impending change of weather, and "guess" correctly where conditions will be more favourable to them.

Salmon, eels and many other creatures perceive from vast distances the most suitable place for spawning, and for the hatching and development of their young.

Yet others, like ants, appear to foresee whether a winter will be hard or mild, and take steps to protect themselves against a greater or a less degree of cold. We could quote a multitude of analogous perceptions among mammals, birds, insects and fish, which have aroused more interest in British and American students of psychical research than in France. They seem to be of a much more "paranormal" character than many of the human phenomena to which this adjective is applied.

More still: human paranormal cognition seems to be very much more highly developed among primitive peoples than in urban industrialized man. Aborigines from Australia, Central Africa, South America, are gifted with a delicacy of hearing, an accuracy of intuition, a vivid telepathic power which leaves our methods of divination and clairvoyance far behind.

Are our paranormal cognitions then anything other than a residuum in civilized man of an animal function which has largely atrophied in consequence of our habitual use of other methods of perception and of exchanging ideas? Robert Amadou considers them to be "survivals of a very primitive mode of consciousness and of action".

There can be no question of envisaging a return to these

primitive forms of awareness in our species as progress. They can be used and exploited to thrill the public with strange experiences—not quite as good as conjuring tricks—but they cannot be considered as a means of enlarging human knowledge.

To analyse and dissect these modes of consciousness and action will have at least one advantage; that of spoiling the game for false mysteries and true mystifiers, and of reducing to their proper proportions those apparently breathtaking gifts which are nevertheless inferior to the instincts of animals.

Our present modes of extra-sensory perception are often very confused and lead to numerous errors. If the phenomena of clairvoyance do sometimes succeed in giving details which correspond to an astonishing degree with the truth, we are nevertheless obliged to recognize that in the vast majority of cases either the clues given are completely false or else the messages are so vague and ambiguous that they are applicable to everyone and to all situations, after the manner of the sybilline oracles.

In radiesthesia too we must posit the same uncertainty of results, and a high proportion of misleading clues. We quote for instance the engineer Luzy of Paris, a well-known radiesthetist, who has been practising this art since 1903. In his book *Une Experience radiesthesique de recherche de disparus* ("A Radiesthetic Experiment in Searching for Missing Persons"), 1953, he writes that the phenomenon of radiesthesia is purely psychical and mental, and that its essential factor is therefore extremely variable. He adds that many diviners do not succeed except when luck or a fortunate coincidence comes their way, and he maintains, speaking of radiesthetists in general, that "the wisest and the most experienced of them know how uncertain the results of radiesthesia are, despite the utmost good will in the cleverest practitioner."

With regard to teleradiesthesia (divining at a distance) the Belgian Committee (C.B.I.S.P.R.P.) published a statement which was of the highest value, coming as it did from M. Georges Discry, President of the International Centre for

Scientific Radiesthesia, of the Academy of Belgian Radiesthetic Sciences and of its federated Circles. He wrote on November 27th, 1945, to the Committee saying: "You have confused radiesthesia and teleradiesthesia, and there is a world of difference between them. Only charlatans use the latter, and they should be exposed."

At the Utrecht conversations Professor Emilio Servadio made the following disappointing statement on the uncertainty of extra-sensory perception: "*Psi* phenomena have little or no influence on the development of our culture. They are in fact very much less useful than the normal means of communication. No one can doubt that a case of telepathy, however striking, is infinitely less convenient and precise than a telephone call or a telegram."

To wind up with Robert Amadou: "The future of mankind does not lie in a return to the infantile behaviour of the species, or in the abandonment of the rational faculties."

PARAPSYCHOLOGY OR CLASSICAL PSYCHOLOGY?

Charles Richet wrote over thirty years ago: "As soon as certain so-called clairvoyant phenomena can be explained by an extreme acuteness of the human intelligence working through systematic subconscious constructions of ideas it is clear that we need no longer call on parapsychology; that is, posit either the existence of unknown faculties in our own minds, or the intervention of other minds." Since then parapsychology has not only discarded numerous phenomena whose existence was only apparent, since they were the effect of illusion, trickery, fraud, conjuring, etc. It has also, in analysing that modicum of evidence which stands up to criticism, and whose authenticity seems to have been established, revealed the preponderant influence of the subconscious mind and of the remains of a primitive function.

Are there really paranormal activities? In showing the part played in them by the subconscious are we not really reintegrating them into classical psychology? Is it not the function of psycho-analysis to descend into the infantile and instinctive depths of the psyche, in a feat of exploration which is really a sort of retreat, a regression towards the most primitive components of human psychology? Will not parapsychology reorientate itself towards a return to normal psychology which will, in the last analysis, work out the true, and perfectly natural explanation of reputedly paranormal phenomena.[1]

Many are the contemporary parapsychologists who show themselves favourable to this supposition.

In his book on Parapsychology, which is at present the most complete and authoritative French study of the subject, Robert Amadou quite frankly takes up this position: "Parapsychology has no right to claim the status of an independent discipline unless it acts either very arbitrarily or in a purely provisional way. . . . While we maintain that parapsychology is a branch of ordinary psychology, we should like to say that the phenomena which form the subject matter of parapsychology will sooner or later be handled by psychology itself."

Psychology does in fact already study some of the phenomena which in especial cases seem to us paranormal, because of concomitant circumstances or striking consequences. Suggestion, autosuggestion, double personality, psychological automatism, unconscious romancing, etc., quite certainly come within the jurisdiction of classical psychology. If, in cases of mediumism, clairvoyance or paranormal healing they take on a more marvellous aspect, apparently superior to the forces of nature, this does not create an unsurmountable barrier, or even a clear line of demarcation, separating them from more ordinary cases.

The same thing holds good of the communication of thought, or extra-sensory perception; can it really be maintained nowadays that these phenomena elude the grasp of classical psychology?

[1] This reads oddly to the English eye, to which there seems to be no necessary antithesis between the natural and the paranormal; the latter is usually supposed to be an unrecognized function of the former. [*Trans.*]

CONCLUSION

A PLEA FOR PARAPSYCHOLOGY

It seems more and more probable, though nevertheless not certain, that the science of parapsychology will become a branch of ordinary psychology. The paranormal will doubtless show itself to be more and more normal in its nature and origins. Must we conclude from this that "the youngest of the sciences dealing with Man" is also the most ephemeral of them?

It should be noted from the first that those scientists whose conclusions about so-called paranormal phenomena are the most negative are cautious as to what they exclude. Almost all psychical research workers today would still endorse the following declaration made in 1932 by Dr Eugène Osty, former President of the International Metapsychical Institute, in his book *Les Pouvoirs inconnus de l'esprit sur la matière* ("The Unknown Powers of the Spirit over Matter"): "We wish, for the sake of the progress of knowledge about life, that the scientific *élite* could get over its preconceived ideas about paranormal psychic powers; ideas which have of course been engendered, nurtured and strengthened by innumerable fraudulent mediums, innumerable inaccurate observations, innumerable rash excursions into print. We should like to persuade them that while it is true that mythomania and dishonesty on the one hand and incompetence and credulity on the other have played some part, even, let us say, an important part in the history of paranormal psychic manifestations, it is none the less true that certain beings are in fact gifted with paranormal powers."

More remarkable still is the reserve of Dr Hougardy, member of the Belgian Committee, C.B.I.S.P.R.P. (described in Chapter I) who laid down very strict conditions for his experimental work, and was extremely negative in the conclusions he drew from it. In the *Archiva Medica Belgica* (1950, vol. 5, p. 7) he maintains: "It would be contrary to the scientific spirit to exclude *a priori* the possibility of new evidence, which might oblige us to review our first judgement. It should be reiterated that our conclusions apply only to the cases and kinds of phenomena said to be paranormal which we ourselves have had the occasion to study. . . . We have not traced any element which could allow us to attribute any psychical or physiological substratum whatever to so-called paranormal activities, or which could weaken the severe verdict of the experts upon the set-backs suffered by 'paranormal persons' in the most varied fields. . . . In short, we have not been able to put any paranormal phenomena on record. But this negative result only sharpens our curiosity. We are ready now, as in the past, to cooperate with everyone of good faith who believes himself to be gifted with a paranormal power, and would agree to experiment in laboratory conditions designed to eliminate all possibility of error, illusion or fraud."

Parapsychology, then, retains its usefulness even for psychologists, who need experts to help them to discard or to elucidate apparently paranormal occurrences which might involve them in unreal problems.

But parapsychology remains a discipline necessary to many other studies.

The researches and publications of parapsychologists are and always will be necessary for the detection and exposure of the fraudulent marvels of fakirs, clairvoyants, mediums, healers, radiesthetists and charlatans of every stamp, when these go beyond all bounds in their shameless exploitation of public credulity.

Assuredly illusion is in part a comfort, a means of escape for those who need to get away from the triviality of life, or who are avid for anything mysterious and strange. Conjurers and illusionists have a rôle which may be relaxing and beneficial. Yogis and healers sometimes do good.

But the wide extent of the publicity given today to all these "paranormal" persons with all their prodigious feats and miracles leads to sinister consequences, which it is urgently necessary to break up. Experience shows that both the laws and the various municipal by-laws against the exploitation of the public are practically useless, as are the various actions taken by the Order of Doctors. Only a scientifically based campaign to show up the fraud and trickery practised by these persons has much chance of opening people's eyes to them, and of reducing the damage they do.

The material consequences of these aberrations are startling enough. In 1935 3,460 offices where clairvoyants could be consulted were registered in Paris alone; their annual income, as declared for tax purposes, amounted to over 73,000,000 francs. Their number has now increased enormously. It is estimated that there are now some 75,000 diviners and clairvoyants of all kinds in France, and that their annual receipts are in the neighbourhood of 750,000,000 francs (roughly $2,000,000.

Who can assess how much money is wasted by industrial or municipal undertakings in the search for underground water or minerals whose presence has been avowed by dowsers? Maître P. Descroix, secretary general of the French Association of Municipal Engineers and Technicians, wrote in the *Archives Belges de Médecine sociale, Hygiène, Médecine du Travail et Médecine Légale* ("Belgian Archives of Social, Industrial and Legal Medicine and Hygiene"), No. 7, 1952: "a chief civil engineer working in rural districts told us recently that in his opinion the employment of a dowser in the search for a water supply for a commune involved on an average in each case the expenditure of a million French francs on useless work".

It is also worth while to bear in mind the enormous expenses to which private individuals or the police commit themselves in following up clues given by dowsers or clairvoyants as to the whereabouts of missing persons or objects.

Parapsychology will have a part to play in the tracking down of those dangerous "healers" who spread distrust of trained medical men, and of officially recognized remedies and methods of treatment, who prevent their dupes from undergoing vitally necessary surgical operations, who rely on "magnetized" medicaments, or who not only cannot cure illness but can and do gravely injure health. Recent lawsuits have shown how often confidence in healers, spiritualist or otherwise, has brought about the death of sick persons who could easily have been cured by orthodox medicine.

Imagine the possible consequences of a formula like this, given in a work on radiesthesis cited by Dr Hougardy:

"Equip your instrument case with a set of transparent cellophane screens of different colours. You should hold out the various screens, one after another, above the source or stream of water that has been found, placing each in turn between the moving pendulum and the surface of the ground. The water will be good to drink if there is a syntony between it and the lilac-violet screen; that is, if the pendulum maintains its regular movements while this screen is in use. The lighter the colour the better the water, which will be less good in accordance with the degree to which you have to use the darker colours. Indigo will show a kind of water which is clearly contra-indicated. Red shows a water containing iron." Should not public malefactors of this kind be brought to book? Parapsychologists should submit samples of water polluted with the organisms of typhoid or poliomyelitis to them.

By educating general opinion, parapsychologists will help to protect the public against the serious psychological and moral consequences of some of the "messages" given by certain types of "psychic".

They will explode the stories put about by various diviners, healers and clairvoyants; stories of sorcerers who stick pins in wax images of their victims, or roast them before a slow fire, thus causing wasting disease and death; stories of "evil absent treatment" and "harmful waves" and stories of the disastrous radiations emitted by geological fissures.

Who can tell how many people these revelations have disturbed to the point of obsession, monomania, paranoia or suicide; or how many have let themselves be drawn into such fierce hatred against "sorcerers" that they have murdered them by poison or other secret methods, which the so-called "sorcerer" would never have suspected in a person to whom in fact he wished nothing but good?

We ought also to mention those "predictions" which bring about idiotic and fatally unhappy marriages, or commit young people to careers for which they are completely unsuited, or induce business men to undertake wonderful speculations which fail lamentably; not forgetting the families estranged and the engagements broken off by clairvoyants, and the despair of those convinced by their horoscopes or by other kinds of fortune-telling that at such and such a date misfortune will inevitably befall them.

We could draw up a long indictment against these sowers of fear, panic, hatred, implacable rancour and groundless suspicion between members of a family, or close friends.

We should perhaps touch on the tragedy of those who, deceived by clairvoyants, believe in a sort of anguished delirium that someone they loved, who was killed long years ago, is still alive. We have seen a mother harassing the highest authorities and continually undertaking expensive journeys abroad because a medium had told her that her officer son (whose dead body had been identified without possibility of error by the personal papers found on it) was still alive, somewhere abroad . . . until the day when the poor woman, thrown off her mental balance by this obsession, had to be certified insane.

Even the police, in certain much-discussed cases, have more than once been deceived by entirely erroneous clues furnished by clairvoyants and radiesthetists into following up false trails, arresting innocent persons and covering them with suspicion, and multiplying inquiries and investigations.

THE RELIGIOUS POINT OF VIEW

As was said in Chapter III, psychical research workers can do a useful service to religion by helping to map out the borderlines between the supernatural, the direct action of God; the paranormal, which may, in spite of its mysterious appearance arise from natural causes; and the phony miracles with which our era abounds.

They can help in the struggle against superstition and occultism, against the preoccupation with the marvellous that can crowd out true religious feeling, and against the damage done to the reputation of true miracles by their ridiculous or illusory imitations.

Men have always needed and will always need serious critical studies of such subjects, eliminating or at any rate reducing the part played by the passion for the extraordinary in the religious make-up of people dominated by sensibility, imagination and morbid curiosity. It is well known that the marvellous, true or false, has a great attraction for neurotic and unbalanced persons. It is only too easy to see how much evil is done by lecturers, and editors of periodicals who are always on the look-out for strange manifestations, absurd miracles, grotesque apparitions, doubtful stigmatics, etc., occurrences which the Church has never endorsed and will be very careful not to endorse since, as Cardinal Ottaviani has said, it is "the enemy of false miracles".

THE SCIENTIFIC POINT OF VIEW

Psychical research also has the advantage of being able to show up, for what they are, the multiplicity of pseudo-scientific publications which introduce their readers to the most inept ideas, degrading the intelligence and engendering an unbelievable silliness. It is extremely important to disabuse the multitude of readers at present gulled by the high-sounding jargon of charlatans who, knowing nothing of physics, chemistry or physiology, yet set out completely incomprehensible "expositions" to dazzle the public, ignorant of scientific terms.

Dr Hougardy, Chief Inspector of Hygiene in Belgium, quotes the following hilarious passage from a book entitled *L'Homme, cet être peu connu, peut apprendre à se mieux connaître* ("Man, that little known Being, can learn to know himself better"). It does indeed make the most unexpected revelations. "The function of the cerebellum is to store up the electro-magnetic waves received through the eye, and the cosmic waves received by the brain following a given order. . . . Another cerebellum, however, is to be found in the interior of the body. This cerebellum is the spleen, which organ forms a sort of accumulator, and serves, reinforces and forms a reserve of some kind for the liver, intestines and genitals." Are not these prodigious discoveries rather dangerous for the normal human brain? The same author refers in this work to "the great lymphatic nervous system" and to the "petentary gland".

A famous exponent of radiesthesia has published the conditions necessary if one is to become a radiesthetist. Here they are: "To be a water-diviner one must have a fluidic sensibility of between 15 and 62 degrees, plus a special circumvolution whose diameter is from 1 to 18 millimetres. There are 22 electric fluids and 4 magnetic fluids. The earth is surrounded by 5 layers of different fluids, whose heights are determined to within a metre. The stratosphere is to be found at a height of 59,962 metres. The body emanations combine with the solar rays and the colours of the spectrum: thus, those of men's bodies have an affinity for red, those of plants for blue, etc. The radiations of a man extend to a height of 25.97 metres, those of a woman to 3 metres less, those of animals to 6.97 metres.[1] Individuals emit to the left of them waves coming from the blood; they extend up to 1,297 metres for a man, and 797 for a woman, etc."

We could quote many other examples of this lunatic literature which is not confined to France.[2] Pity human intelligence!

As well as liberating man from unjustified fears, and protecting him from being misled by mumbo-jumbo, psychical research can enrich psychology. In plumbing the moving deeps of the subconscious, analysing the primitive instincts of extra-sensory perception and testing the obscure reflex activities of our nature, these studies can be of use to classical psychology, throwing light on phenomena still imperfectly understood.

For these reasons, even if the paranormal must in the end be seen as an aspect of the normal not yet fully explored,[3] parapsychology will retain its usefulness and its claim to exist as a specialized branch of research. Let us hope that, liberated from all those prejudices, which in the past have often vitiated its conclusions, it will develop on lines that are strictly scientific and completely objective.

[1] Mice and elephants alike, apparently. [*Trans.*]

[2] The translator was assured, in England some years ago, that if she gave three drops of her blood to a woman with an electrical machine, the latter would tune into her wavelength at a certain time of day and transmit healing vibrations which could be received by standing barefoot on open ground anywhere.

[3] Thus leading to a larger concept of the norm. [*Trans.*]

SELECT BIBLIOGRAPHY

Note.—As far as I know, the only Catholic authors to be found in this list are the late Fr Herbert Thurston, S.J., and his editor, Fr J. H. Crehan, S.J. The reason is that until now Catholics in the English-speaking world do not seem to have taken much interest in the subject from the scientific point of view. Fr A. A. Stephenson, S.J., whose admirable contribution to *The Month* may be remembered, has so far produced nothing in book form.

For the most part the authors cited here handle their material from a point of view akin to that of the biologist, observing, experimenting and formulating and testing hypotheses as to what goes on and why. There is little need to apprehend the danger of which Fr Reginald Omez is vividly aware: that of trespass into the field of theology. Professor Broad and Professor H. H. Price have each used the data of psychical research in work on philosophical themes, but it is unnecessary to list their books in a volume designed for the general reader. For the rest, Catholics may sometimes find a blind ignorance of their beliefs (as in Dr West's curious comments on the poltergeist phenomena in the life of the Curé d'Ars) and an occasional preconception which they cannot share; but in general the theme is handled from a neutral and objective point of view.

The late J. W. Dunne's books exemplify the inquiry into the nature of time to which psychical research must give rise. Dr Bendit's essay, written as a thesis for a doctorate, describes paranormal phenomena encountered in the course of his medical work. Dr C. S. Lewis, the distinguished Anglican, has produced one of the cleverest and most readable studies of miracles to appear in contemporary England. Dr Moncrieff's book discusses from an oculist's point of view the theory that the senses canalize perception, enabling the mind to select only the relevant items in the bewildering flow of paranormal cognition which would otherwise pour incessantly in upon our attention. Ronald Edwin describes, as an articulate guinea-pig, those extra-sensory experiences which led him to adopt and later, in the cause of truth, to abandon, the career of a spiritualist medium; and Ronald Rose's fascinating document recounts his field work in psychical research among Australian aborigines. The titles of the rest are self-explanatory.

BARRETT, SIR W. F.: *Psychical Research*, London, Home University Library, 1911.

BENDIT, LAURENCE, M.D.: *Paranormal Cognition*, London, Faber, 1944.

CARINGTON, WHATELEY: *Telepathy* (2nd ed.), London, Methuen and New Haven, Conn., Yale Univ. Press, 1945.

CREHAN, J. H., S.J.: *Father Thurston*, London and New York, Sheed and Ward, 1952.

DINGWALL, Dr E. and LANGDON-DAVIES, J.: *The Unknown, is it Nearer?* London, Cassell, and New York, New American Library, 1956.

DUNNE, J. W.: *An Experiment with Time* (3rd ed.), London, Faber, and New York, Macmillan, 1934; *The Serial Universe*, London, Faber, and New York, Macmillan, 1934.

EDWIN, RONALD: *Clock without Hands*, London, Sidgwick and Jackson, and New York, Wehman, 1955.

EHRENWALD, Dr JAN: *Telepathy and Medical Psychology*, London, Allen and Unwin, 1947.

FLEW, ANTONY: *A New Approach to Psychical Research*, London, Watts, 1953.

GURNEY, E. and PODMORE, F. (Ed. Mrs Henry Sidgwick): *Phantasms of the Living* (abridged ed.), London, Kegan Paul, 1918.

LEWIS, Dr C. S.: *Miracles*, London, Bles, and New York, Macmillan, 1947.

MONCRIEFF, Dr M. M.: *The Clairvoyant Theory of Perception*, London, Faber, and New York, Harper, 1951.

RHINE, Dr J. B.: *Extra Sensory Perception*, Boston, Mass., 1934; *New Worlds of the Mind*, London, Faber, and New York, Sloane, 1955; *Telepathy and Human Personality* (Myers Memorial Lecture), London, S.P.R., 1951.

ROSE, RONALD: *Living Magic*, London, Chatto and Windus, and Chicago, Rand McNally, 1957.

SALTER, W. H.: *The Society for Psychical Research: an Outline of its History*, London, S.P.R., 1948.

SOAL, S. G., D.Sc.: *The Experimental Situation* (Myers Memorial Lecture), London, S.P.R., 1948.

SOAL, S. G. and BATEMAN, F.: *Modern Experiments in Telepathy*, London, Faber, and New Haven, Conn., Yale Univ. Press, 1954.

THOULES, ROBERT H., Ph.D.: *Psychical Research Past and Present* (Myers Memorial Lecture), London, S.P.R., 1948.

THURSTON, HERBERT, S.J. (ed. J. H. Crehan, S.J.): *The Physical Phenomena of Mysticism*, London, Burns Oates, and Chicago, Regnery, 1953; *Ghosts and Poltergeists*, London, Burns Oates, 1953; *Surprising Mystics*, London, Burns Oates, and Chicago, Regnery, 1954.

TYRRELL, G. N. M.: *Science and Psychical Phenomena*, London, Methuen, 1938; *The Personality of Man*, London and Baltimore, Penguin Books; *Apparitions* (revised edition with a preface by H. H. Price), London, Duckworth, and New York, Pantheon, 1953.

WEST, Dr D. J.: *Tests for Extra Sensory Perception* (revised ed.), S.P.R., London, 1954; *Psychical Research Today*, London, Duckworth, 1954, and New York, Macmillan, 1955.